ROMAN POETRY

ROMAN POETRY

FROM THE REPUBLIC
TO THE SILVER AGE

TRANSLATED AND
WITH INTRODUCTIONS BY
DOROTHEA WENDER

SOUTHERN ILLINOIS UNIVERSITY PRESS
Carbondale

Printed in the United States of America

Library of Congress Cataloging-in-Publication Data
Roman Poetry: from the Republic to the Silver Age / translated and
    with introductions by Dorothea Wender.
        p. cm.
    1. Latin poetry—Translations into English. 2. English poetry—
Translations from Latin. 1. Wender, Dorothea, 1934–.
PA6164.R63   1991
874'0108—dc20   90-9808
ISBN 0-8093-1694-3 (paper)   CIP
ISBN 978-0-8093-1694-6 (paper)

20   19   18   17   9   8   7   6

For Chase and B

CONTENTS

PREFACE

There are many ways of dividing up classics professors (should you ever by chance feel impelled to do so); there are the historians and the literary critics (to say nothing of the philosophers, archaeologists, linguists, epigraphists, prosopographers), the teachers and the writers, those who love Achilles and those who loathe Achilles, the young and the old, the unemployed and the tenured, and so forth. But one of the sharpest divisions among them is that between Hellenists and Latinists, or students of Greece versus those of Rome. Hellenists, it is said, are Democrats; Latinists vote Republican. Hellenists have longer hair; Latinists wear three-piece suits. Hellenists are enthusiastic about Big Ideas; Latinists grow warm over fine points of style. Hellenists are perpetual adolescents; Latinists were born middle-aged. The clever reader no doubt gets the idea.

Does this division tell us anything about differences between the ancient Greeks and Romans? Are these professors anything like the subjects they choose to study? Yes, in a general and oversimplified way, they are. The Greeks had great genius, vitality, originality, ingenuity, and subtlety, but they often messed things up terribly. They invented tragedy, comedy, history, democracy, and philosophy (all more or less in the same century, too—the fifth B.C.), but it took the Romans to develop a really workable sewer system and central heating.

The Romans were also very good at business, and at the administration of large and complicated groups, like armies and nations. They hit on the idea of putting snow in their drinks, to keep their wine chilled. They worried about body odor a good deal, bathed frequently, and wore perfume. Their ideals were "masculine," and they were more self-consciously manly than the "soft" Greeks, but they fell in love with women, often behaved like perfect asses about them, and actually let some of them share their lives. They believed passionately in what they called *gravitas* (seriousness, dignity)—and produced first-rate silly farces. They were prudish about sex, nudity, and bodily functions—and wrote better pornography and viler obscene humor than the Greeks did. They worshiped authority (literally, sometimes)—and bred some wonderfully sly antiauthoritarian poets. They were gourmets—and felt guilty about their obsession with food. They loved violence—and felt guilty about that, too. Above all, they loved money, luxury, and comfort—and never tired of praising the simple, poor farmers of the past.

In short, the Romans were American. Most Americans today, who encounter ancient Greece with reverent awe, or irritated puzzlement, or admiring amazement, feel right at home with the Romans. Even their portrait busts look just like Wall Street brokers or Milwaukee real estate agents.

Most literary works of the Romans, frankly, do not come anywhere near the dazzling heights set by their Greek predecessors. Roman epic (Virgil, Lucan, Statius) does not; Roman tragedy (Seneca) certainly does not. The early Roman comedies of Plautus and Terence are often wonderful and funny, but not enough of the Greek comedies they imitated survive for us to make a comparison. In philosophy, no Roman could compete with Plato or Aristotle, and few tried. The histories of the Romans Sallust, Caesar, Livy, and Tacitus are all worth reading, but none has the scope and charm of Herodotus or the sober, logical brilliance of Thucydides. With regard to oratory and rhetoric, a case could be made for the superiority of Cicero to the Greek Demosthenes, but this is not a genre we appreciate much now. Only in the formal poetic satire—a genre invented by the Romans—and in lyric poetry can we say with confidence that the Romans gave the world something new, lasting, precious, which actually improved on the extant work of the Greeks.

This volume includes what I think is the best of that poetry. I have not included any epic or drama; they need to be presented whole. I have omitted a few figures who are historically important (like Ennius, the father of Latin literature, and Lucilius, the first important satirist) and some who have their fans but are generally classed as minor (like the satirist Persius and the witty Petronius who wrote some poetry but is chiefly known for his prose novel *The Satyricon*.) Even so, I have had to leave out many excellent poems by the authors I include, and no doubt I will from now on be attacked for having had the nerve to omit this while including that. A few poems in this book are included chiefly because they are famous or historically interesting. All the others are here because I like them.

METER

The Romans borrowed all their meters from the Greeks. Classical Latin poetry, like the Greek, never rhymes, and its rhythms do not depend on regularly arranged stress accents, as in English, but on the length of time for which a syllable is pronounced (Eng. WASH-ing-ton vs. Lat. C y n -thi-a). Although we can write English verses that approximate Latin meters or are roughly equivalent to them, they can never really sound the same. In my translations I have sometimes tried to imitate or approximate the originals (for example in Catullus *Songs* 1, 2, 3, 8, 11, and 51), substituting stressed syllables for "long" ones. More often, though, I have used familiar English meters (blank verse, ballad meter, heroic couplets, an occasional sonnet, and some mixed types of my own devising). My aim in every case was to try to reproduce the effect or tone of the original form, not its precise meter. That excludes free verse (poetic prose): These Latin poems are all very formal—however modern their thoughts—and I think they require conventional verse forms to preserve their elegant music. I have used rhyme whenever I thought it would be appropriate.

GENRES

A variety of poetic genres are represented here. First, there is *lyric* (Catullus, the *Odes* of Horace, some of Martial). These are generally short, personal poems, written in a variety of meters. A subspecies of *lyric* is *elegy* (the latter poems of Catullus, all of Propertius and Tibullus, the love poems of Ovid, most of Martial). The elegiac meter is a couplet form: odd-numbered lines are dactylic hexameter; even-numbered lines (pentameters) fall into two short halves. In spite of its popularity in the ancient world, it is an odd meter to our ears; each couplet ends with two abrupt and rather jarring breaks (after each half of the pentameter line). I have tried to devise a roughly equivalent meter for English; you will find it used in Propertius, Tibullus, Ovid, and some of Catullus. Martial's witty epigrams, though, seem to me to cry out for plain old English ballad meter, with rhymes to bring out the punch lines. Long *didactic* poems (here represented by Lucretius and Virgil's *Georgics*) were generally written in dactylic hexameter by both Greeks and Romans. It is, for their languages, the smoothest, easiest, and best meter for long works, for *epic*, for *didactic* poetry, and for *long narratives* like Ovid's collection of short stories, the *Metamorphoses*. *Satires*, too, were generally written in the epic meter. In English, the equivalent meter, clearly, is blank verse (unrhymed iambic pentameter), and I have accordingly used it for these works. Another genre that uses dactylic hexameter is the *pastoral* (Virgil's *Eclogues*); I have used blank verse for *Eclogues* 4, but for *Eclogues* 2 I tried something different.

SUBJECT MATTER

Many different subjects are treated by the Roman poets, more than modern poets find appropriate. There are, of course, the poet's old standbys—love, death, and the return of spring. But there is also serious philosophy, social criticism, literary criticism, physics, history, and agriculture. There is surprisingly little description of the beauties of nature, even in pastoral, and even in those many poems that treat at length the superiority of country life to the city, the "view" is scarcely noticed; people, their emotions, and their behavior are what chiefly interest these poets, and what make their poetry interesting even now. The emotion of hatred receives particularly full treatment—passionate, unabashed hatred for institutions, for classes, and especially for specific individuals, who are often mentioned by name. Roman poetry is not soft, even if it is, often, pretty. The Roman poets lived in a time when the poet still had power (real power, like that of a TV producer today, not just something mystical). In fact the power of song was one of their favorite topics, and the power to curse was valued no less highly than the power to bless or the power to seduce.

STYLE

Not much needs to be said here about style. The Roman poets had it, were obsessed with it, knew all about it. They loved words, and playing with words, and they were lucky to have a musical language in which to write. They did not have the great original ideas of the Greeks. But they were thorough professionals who knew just how to achieve the effects they wanted to produce.

TRANSLATION

A good verse translation (I first said this elsewhere) should do four things. It should be faithful to its original in content; it should be faithful in tone (or manner, or effect); it should be accessible to the modern reader; it should be a good poem in itself. These four requirements obviously conflict with each other sometimes. For example, in order to be faithful in tone to most Latin lyrics, a formal meter should be used. But formal meter makes it much harder to be precisely faithful in content. (You can be sure that almost any rhymed, metrical translation will be less literal than any free verse or prose rendition.) And what is content, anyway? Are the metaphors used by a poet part of his essential content, or are they merely decorative? Generally, I think they *are* part of the essential content, especially in

Latin poetry, where style is often more important than ideas. But you see the problem. Then, consider the criterion of accessibility. If a poet says "the Spartan wife" when he means Helen of Troy, the modern reader may not know whom he is talking about. Should the translator say "Helen" and lose faithfulness in manner as well as content, or should she or he say "the Spartan wife" and put in an irritating footnote? This sort of problem comes up in nearly every poem; those ancients knew a lot of mythology (and other things) that we do not know, and they did not often choose to say things in the simplest way possible. I have tried to balance the claims of all four criteria as well as I could, but inevitably, there will be some or many who will feel my choices were mistaken. With the fourth criterion (that the translation itself be a good poem) I had the least problem. These are all good poems; I have not been tempted to rewrite or improve on them; I have simply tried to write, in their manner, as well as I could. If the results are not pleasing, it is my fault; if they are, the credit should go to the original poets.

TEXTS

I have based my translations on the Oxford Classical Texts, except in the brief selection from Ovid's *Metamorphoses* for which the text I used was that of D. E. Bosselaar (The Netherlands: Brill, Leiden, 1968). In Catullus (*Songs*), poem 25, I omitted line 5, which is impossible; in poem 39, I read *parcus* for *pinguis*; in poem 51, I supply *vocis in ore* for the missing line 8. In Lucretius's *De Rerum Natura*, book 1, I have restored the old lines 44–49; in book 2, I omit line 43a; in book 3, line 853, I substitute *neque* for *nil*. In Martial *Epigrams* 10.65, *ilia* is much funnier than *filia*. Generally I have tried to avoid including poems whose texts are very uncertain.

I have many people to thank for their help. First, Luciana Hnatt, my inspiring first Latin teacher, who introduced me to Horace and Ovid and taught me to love their language. Next, my friends and colleagues—all better Latinists than I—James and Susanna Zetzel, Jennifer Roberts, Judith Hallett, John Sullivan, Robert Tannenbaum, and Charles Henderson. The Zetzels ought to be particularly singled out: They lent me books and gave me good counsel, encouragement, and the warmth of their friendship in a particularly cold year. Next, my daughters Jocelyn, Leslie, and Melissa, who read and liked some of the poems, who cheered when I finished things, and who were very patient about all this. Wheaton College has been good to me, and good for me. Princeton University, too, has been kind enough to let me use its facilities for a year. I would also like to acknowledge the

Classical Journal for permission to reprint my verse translations of Horace *Odes* 1.11 and 1.22, which were originally published in the October 1958 issue (vol. 54, no. 1, pp. 20, 24). Finally, it would be rather fun to dedicate the book to "Lesbia, Corinna, Delia, and Cynthia, who were immortalized but never got to tell *their* side," but a closer bond impels me to present this offering, instead, to my loved brothers.

POETS OF THE
ROMAN
REPUBLIC

CATULLUS

W. B. Yeats's fine poem about scholars and poets ("Bald heads forgetful of their sins . . .") serves as a healthy warning to all us poor, bloodless souls who study and translate and teach the works not only of Catullus but of any lyric poet. It is tempting to omit the introduction altogether and say, simply, "read these good poems." (But undoubtedly my clever reader knows that this temptation will, somehow, be mastered.)

The facts we know about the poet's life are scanty. His name was Gaius Valerius Catullus. He was born in Verona, of a good and probably rich family, in about 84 B.C. Sometime in his twenties he moved to Rome, where he became a friend (or enemy) of many of the important political and literary figures of the day, including the great orator, writer, and statesman Cicero (friend, probably), Julius Caesar (enemy, then perhaps friend), the tribune and political thug Clodius Pulcher (probably friend, then enemy), the historian and biographer Cornelius Nepos (friend), the poet and orator Licinius Calvus (friend), and the statesman Memmius, to whom the great work of Lucretius is dedicated (boss, then enemy.) In 57 B.C., when Memmius went to Bithynia as propraetor (governor), Catullus went along, on his staff. During this period in Asia, he visited the grave of his brother, near Troy.

The chief event in the poet's life, however, at least from the standpoint of his poetry, was his love affair, in Rome, with Clodia, probably the sister of Clodius Pulcher and the wife, then widow, of Q. Metellus Celer, a prominent politician. Clodia was beautiful and sophisticated and seems to have attracted nearly every man in Rome (to such a degree that it would be surprising if Yeats's phrase "beauty's ignorant ear" really fit her case)—including the high-minded Cicero, who later tore her to shreds in an unfair, spiteful, and wickedly funny criminal-court oration, *Pro Caelio*. Catullus fell in love with Clodia, and called her "Lesbia" ("woman of Lesbos") after the famous, passionate Greek poet Sappho, who was a native of that island. Catullus elevated his love for Clodia into something quite new, quite different from the usual Greek (and early Roman) relationship found in poetry before his time. He wanted his love to be a bond between equals—a "treaty," he calls it. He thought that bond might last a long time, perhaps forever. He felt that romantic love might, at best, even be similar to the feelings one has for the members of one's family. None of these ideas seems very startling to us as products of the Christian *cum* women's magazine *cum* Hollywood tradition of Love. But the typical Greek love affair was between unequals—freeman with courtesan or adult man with boy. The man, who wrote the poems, pretended that he was a "slave" to the charms of his beloved; he was always the wooer and giver of gifts; the beloved (boy or whore) was not really expected to love in return, but merely to yield up his/her "favors" in return for the gifts and the poems and so forth; the understanding was that the affair would be transitory and could not last beyond the beloved's loss of youth and beauty. In this tradition, then, Catullus's feelings for Clodia seem quite unusual, even "unmanly" (see poem 16 for that accusation). At any rate, Catullus wrote his best poems for Clodia and later—when her chronic infidelity was established—against Clodia. Sometime after 55 B.C., probably at about the age of thirty, Catullus died.

Only one manuscript of his poems survived, and in some places the text is still dubious. The work falls into three parts. The first section consists chiefly of short poems in various lyric meters, not arranged chronologically. The second part contains longer poems, of which "The Wedding of Peleus and Thetis" is the longest and most elegantly constructed. The third section is a collection of short poems in the elegiac meter. All the poems I have included here are from the first and third parts. All three sections show some influence of Greek poetry, particularly from the third-century Alexandrian period, an age in which poets valued brevity, cleverness, polish, erudition, and romance. But Catullus was one of the great lyric poets in history, and it is a mistake to become too obsessed with precisely what he borrowed from whom. His work surpasses that of any Greek lyricist we possess.

There is a wide range of tone, emotion, and technique in his work: he can be tender, witty, erotic, hysterically angry, delicately tactful, childishly smutty, thoughtful, innocent, learned, artful and "artless." Sometimes his most terrific effects come from a violent clash of tones within one poem; in number 11, for example, the formal, polished, pompous first lines build up to the presentation of his "brief and not pretty" message to Lesbia. The gross vileness of that message, in the midst of such civilized surroundings, is like a handful of excrement in the face—and then he turns around again and ends the poem with the delicate, pretty image of his love as a flower at the meadow's edge, cut down by the relentless, unfeeling machine that is Lesbia.

Catullus often seems—particularly when compared with the other great Roman lyricist, Horace—to be entirely "natural," spontaneous, sincere, the perfect archetype of Yeats's hot young man, tossing in his bed, "rhyming out" line after line in a white-hot blaze of passion. Certainly, this is the effect he produces, and we have no right to assume that he did not really feel all those emotions as strongly as he expressed them. But it is good to remember, too, that all of his poems—even those that read like schoolboy graffiti—were composed in elegant, formal meters, in correct Latin, and were written down on tablets, with the expectation that they would be read by the public. They are not spontaneous cries of rage and desire howled directly into the ears of the parties addressed. Number 5, for example, seems at first like an impulsive, "natural" love poem. But it is most subtly constructed: Words connected with counting run through the poem, which presents, throughout, a contrast between young lovers, who do not count their kisses, and the stuffy, old, prudish, typical business-minded Roman, who views everything, even love, with the eyes of an accountant. The poet's attack on carefulness and calculation is both calculating and careful.

But enough. Read these good poems.

SONGS

1

Who now ought to receive the dedication
In this new pretty book of verses, polished
Smooth with pumice? Cornelius, you're the one, for [1]
It was you at the start who thought my little
Word games really were something to consider,
You who then were the only one who dared to
Set out all of Italian history, three scrolls
Long, yet learned, by Jupiter, and full of
Hard work. Have for yourself whatever pleases
You to take from this little book, and may it
Last, O Patroness Muse, beyond my lifetime.

2

Sparrow, pet and delight of my beloved,
Holding you to her breasts, she loves to tease you,
Loves to offer her fingertip, and tempt you
Angrily to attack with painful pecking,
Any time it amuses her, my shining
Sweetheart, when she could use a bit of joking
Or, I hope, when she needs a little solace
For her pain, to relieve her glowing love pangs;
How I wish I could toy with you, as she does,
And relieve all my soul's most heavy burdens!

3

Mourn and wail, O ye Venuses and Cupids!
Mourn, ye men of affection and refinement!
He is dead, my beloved's favorite sparrow,
Dead, the pet and delight of my beloved
Whom she valued, she said, beyond her eyesight.
He was sweeter than honey, and he knew her
As my lady herself knew her own mother,
Never flying away from her soft bosom

1. Cornelius—Cornelius Nepos, friend of Catullus and acquaintance of Cicero, wrote biographies of famous men, some of which survive, as well as the lost history mentioned here.

He contented himself with hopping round her
Here and there, always peeping to his mistress.
Now he travels along that shady highway
To the region from which there's no returning.
You damned shadows of Orcus, damn you! You take[2]
Everything that is pretty, and devour it:
Now you've taken away my pretty sparrow.
Foully done! O my wretched little sparrow
Now because of your death my sweetheart's charming
Eyes are swollen and small and red with weeping.

5

Let's live, my Lesbia, and let's make love
And let us value all the gossip of
Prudent old men at pennies. When the sun
Sets he can rise again; when we have done
For good and all with our one little light
We sleep forever in one dawnless night.
Give me a thousand kisses, then a hundred,
Another thousand, then a second hundred,
Then still another thousand, then a hundred,
Then, when our number's countless, then, my dear,
Scramble the abacus! So we won't fear
The evil eye of hate, for no one bad
Must know how many kisses we have had.

8

Poor fool Catullus, stop this dumb behavior,
What's lost is lost; you might as well admit it.
There was a time—all suns shone brightly then—
When you were used to going any place where
The Girl commanded, she, so loved by me that
No girl will ever be so loved again.
Then, among jokes and play, things used to happen
Which you desired, nor was she undesiring,
All suns shone brightly on you then, for sure.
Now she says no. You too, you weakling, say it,
Don't chase a fugitive, don't live in anguish,
Be hardened, toughen up your mind, endure.

2. Orcus—the underworld, or the god of the underworld.

Goodbye, my girl. Catullus now is hardened,
He will no longer ask for you nor want you
When you're unwilling; you will be sorry, *you*,
When no one wants you. Slut! What life is waiting
For you, poor thing? Who'll come to you? To what man
Will you seem pretty? Who'll be your lover? Who
Will claim you're his? Who now will get your kisses,
Whose lips your bite? But you, my friend Catullus,
Be hardened and enduring now, stay true.

1 1

Furius: friend Aurelius: devoted comrades,
Both prepared to journey wherever I go
If I go to India's furthest limits
And to the beaches

Where the Dawn's far-echoing waves are pounding,
To Hyrcania, or to the girlish Arabs,
Or among the Scythians, or the archer
Parthians, or that

Valley which the sevenfold Nile has blackened.
Ready, too, to climb up the Alps and visit
Sites of Caesar's greatness, the Gaulish Rhine and
Terrible Channel

And the far-off Britons: my friends, I ask you
Only that you journey to my beloved.
Give her this brief message from me, I beg you,
Brief and not pretty:

Let her live and thrive with her crown of studs
Embracing all three hundred at once, and truly
Loving none, but draining and crushing all their
Manly equipment.

Let her look no more for the love I gave her
Love which, through her fault, like a meadow flower
Fell and withered, nicked by the plow, unthinking
As it was passing.

13

Soon, if the gods are good to you, Fabullus,
You'll have a sumptuous dinner with Catullus,
A splendid meal! Just bring a lot of food,
A pretty girl, some wine, a joking mood,
And lots of laughs. If you bring these, my friend,
You'll feast; *I* haven't any cash to spend,
My purse is full of cobwebs. But you'll get
Essence of Love from me, or sweeter yet
(If anything's more sweet): I mean I have
An elegant gift for you, some perfumed salve,
A present from my lady (and, between us,
I think *she* must have got it straight from Venus)
When you smell this, you'll strike a pious pose
And pray to be transformed into a Nose.

16

I'll bugger you, Aurelius Swishy-tail,
I'll shove it down your throat, Queen Furius!
Because I've written poetry which seems
"A little soft"—you think I'm queer like you.
A poet and his verse are different things:
He should be decent, but his poetry
Need not. His verses, if they're rather "soft"
Or shocking, and are able to excite
The readers' itchy parts, have wit and charm
Not for the little boys, but hairy men
Who don't know how to swish their tails like you.
I write of many thousand kisses—you
Read it, and think that I'm effeminate:
I'll bugger you; I'll shove it down your throats!

25

Gay Thallus, soft as bunny fur or goosedown (and much sweeter)
You're soft as a little earlobe, or an old man's limping peter,
(Dusty from lack of use), and yet, you're devastating, too,
For like a hurricane, you snatch up everything in view;
Return my coat to me, give back the Spanish handkerchief
And my Thynian writing tablets, the engraved ones, you dumb
    thief!

Stop flaunting them in public like your family property,
Unglue them from your fingers, friend, and send them back to me,
Or you'll get *your* engravings, on your soft butt, with a whip,
Your dainty hands will burn with blows, and like a little ship
On the big sea, astonished, you will heave and toss with pain
Because *you* have been caught, my friend, by an angry hurricane!

32

My sweetest Ipsithilla, dear,
My cutie, I implore,
Ask me to come at noon, and sweetie,
Please don't lock the door.

Be right at home and waiting for me,
There's no time to lose,
I want you to be ready, pet,
For nine continuous screws.

I've had my lunch, I'm lying down
And think that I should mention
My tunic *and* my pallium
Are standing at attention.

39

Egnatius has such pearly teeth
He's smiling all the time.
He goes to court; some orator
Describes a heinous crime,
The crown is moved to passion, but
He's smiling all the while,
There's weeping at a funeral:
What does he do but smile?
He smiles at everything. I think
It is a foul disease,
It isn't cosmopolitan
It really doesn't please.

Take warning, good Egnatius! If
You had been born in Rome
Or if you were a Sabine or
If Tibur was your home,
If you were a stingy Umbrian,

A fat Etruscan man,
A toothy, black Lanuvian
Or Transpadane (my clan)
Or any hygienic sort
Whose habits are not vile
I still don't think that I would want
To see you *always* smile.
Of all inanities there are
There's nothing more inane
Than empty smiling. And, what's worse
My friend, you come from Spain.

And Spaniards use their urine
As a handy dentifrice,
So when your smile is bright, we know
That you've been drinking piss!

42

Hendecasyllables, all of you, come to me,[3]
Come to me, all of you, tools of my trade,
I've been robbed of some tablets with poetry on 'em—
Am I to be mocked by a dirty old jade?

Come, let us chase her, and get her to give them up,
"Which is the female?" you ask of me, "which?"
That tart over there, with the grace of an ox
And a ludicrous grin, like a Gallican bitch.

Let us encircle and make our demand of her:
"Give back our tablets, you rotten old bawd!
Give 'em back, rotten bawd, give us back all the tablets!"
We seem to have failed; she is not really awed.

Livelier language will have to be utilized:
"Sewage!" or "Cesspool of evils!" or worse;
It still doesn't budge her, it's still not sufficient,
How *can* we devise a result-getting verse?

Force her, the wanton, to blush with embarrassment,
Chant it in accents more forceful and broad:
"You rotten old bawd, give us back all the tablets,
Hand over the tablets, you rotten old bawd!"

3. Hendecasyllable—an eleven-syllable line, basis of one of Catullus's favorite meters.

MORAL:

Nothing will come of this mode of approaching her,
Here's what wins over the brazen-faced jade,
You must alter your method, to get what you're seeking:
"Pray hand me those tablets, dear modest young maid."

46

Now spring has thawed the Asian winter's chill,
Soft Western breezes, bringing warmth and gladness
Have silenced all the equinoctial madness
Of heaven; now the furious storms grow still.
It's time to leave the Phrygian plains at last,
And all the fertile countryside, to flee
Muggy Nicaea; we'll take wings and see
The glorious cities of the Asian past.
Now, now! my mind is quivering to try
The wandering we've thought about so long,
My happy feet feel restless, ready, strong;
Dear fellow members of the staff, goodbye!
Last year, together, we set out from home,
Now separate paths will bring us back to Rome.

49

Most eloquent of Romulus' descendants,
Of those who are, and were, and who will be
In later ages, Marcus Tullius,[4]
Catullus sends you greatest thanks, Catullus,
Worst of all poets, to the same degree
As, among patrons, you are best of all.

50

Calvus, since we felt lazy yesterday[5]
It suited us to lie around and play
Games with my tablets. It provided sport
For us to write light verses, in one sort

4. Marcus Tullius—M. T. Cicero, the famous orator and statesman.
5. Calvus—C. Licinius Calvus, an orator and poet, also addressed in poem
96.

Of meter, then another, you one line
And I the second, joking, drinking wine.
We had good fun. I came away from it
Licinius, in such fever from your wit
And gaiety, that food could not appease
My hunger, nor did sleep come down to ease
My aching eyes; I crazily tossed all night
All over the bed, longing to see the light,
To be with you again and talk. Half-dead
At last, my limbs lay torpid on the bed
Tired out from all their work, and in the end
I made this poem for you, my happy friend,
So you could learn my sorrow. Now beware
Of pride, my love; do not despise my prayer
Or Nemesis might hurt you. Listen to me:[6]
She's savage; you should treat her reverently.

51

He appears the equal of gods, or even
(May I speak so strongly?) he seems superior
To the gods, who, sitting beside you, often
Sees you and hears you

Gently laugh. That snatches away my senses
Wretched as I am, for when I catch sight of
Lesbia, I'm struck totally mute, I have no
Voice any longer,

And my tongue gets sluggish, throughout my muscles
Runs the quick thin flame, and my ears are clanging
While my eyes' twin lights are extinguished by the
Darkness of nightfall.[7]

6. Nemesis—goddess of vengeance.
7. This poem is almost a literal translation of the first three stanzas of a celebrated Greek poem by Sappho. Immediately after Catullus's version, in our manuscripts, there is one more stanza, in the same (Sapphic) meter: "Idleness [or "leisure"], Catullus, is harmful to you; you go wild in your idleness and play too much. Before now, idleness has destroyed both kings and rich cities." Some scholars think that this stanza must be part of poem 51; I believe it is a fragment of another poem, which was inserted here because of its meter.

58

Caelius, did you know that Lesbia
Our Lesbia, my Lesbia, uniquely
Loved by Catullus, more than his own self
More than his family, now in the crossroads
And alleys, peels the bark back from the rods
Of any offspring of Rome's great-souled founder?

69

You wonder, Rufus, why no girl gives you
Her tender thighs to lie on,
Though you try to melt her with brilliant gems
And filmy gowns to try on,

A fable is hurting you: it says
In the valley beneath your arms
Dwells a wild he-goat. They're all afraid;
The beast has very few charms.

No pretty girl will go to bed
With a beast like that. So, please,
Either kill that stinking pest, or stop
Asking why everyone flees.

72

You used to say you knew only Catullus,
And even Jupiter
Himself could never tempt you.
I valued you, not as males do their females,
But as a father prizes
His sons, and sons-in-law.
Now, Lesbia, I know you. Though I burn
Extravagantly, now,
You are less dear, more cheap.
Such fraud as you have practised makes a lover
"Love" all the more, but not
Wish his beloved well.

75

My mind, my Lesbia, has been dragged down
So far, through you, and has
So lost itself, for you,
I could not like a perfect Lesbia now
Nor could you kill my love
If you did Everything.

76

If it is any pleasure to remember
Good deeds now past, when a man
Thinks he behaved with honor,
And never damaged any trust, nor used
The gods' great name to cheat
Anyone in a pact,
Then many joys are stored for you, Catullus,
For all your life, from this
Disastrous love of yours.
Whatever good a human being can do
Or say, to anyone,
Was done and said by you;
All lost and worthless now, entrusted to
A thankless heart. Why then
Be tortured any more?
Why not be hardened, pull away, and end
This wretchedness, since clearly
The gods do not approve?
Oh, it is difficult to put away
A long love, in a moment;
Difficult, but you must.
This is your only hope: to win a total
Victory. Do it, even
If it's impossible.
O Gods, if you are merciful, if ever
You brought your help to one
At the very edge of death,
Look on me in my sorrow; if my life
Has been lived honorably,
Then take away this plague,
Snatch this calamity away from me.

But, oh, such numbness, creeping
Deep in my joints, expels
All joy from every corner of my heart.
I do not ask that she
Should love me in return,
Or—the impossible—that she should want
To be my faithful lover.
I only pray to be
Well again, and to be relieved of this
Obscene disease. Help me
O Gods, repay my faith.

84

Arrius said "hadvantage" for
"Advantage," and for "ambush",
He thought it most grandiloquent
To shout, distinctly, "*Hambush!*"
He got the trait from Mother
And her various relations;
Her parents, her free brother,
All had great aspirations.

He went abroad, to Syria,
We thought that we were blessed;
Language was soft and smooth again,
Our ears had a nice long rest.
When suddenly the frightening news
Arrived that since our man
Had crossed the Ionian Sea, it was
Now called "HIONIAN."

85

I hate and love. You ask how this can be;
I don't know, that it's true
I know, and I am tortured.

87

No woman can claim honestly that she
Has ever been so loved

As Lesbia by me.
No treaty signer has remained so true
To terms, as I have been
In this love pact with you.

93

Caesar: I'm not so keen on pleasing you,
Nor do I give a damn
Whether you're white or black.

96

If any sweetness, any satisfaction
Deriving from our grief
Can touch the silent tomb
When we in longing, Calvus, love again
Old loves, and weep for those
Friendships long lost to us,
Then surely your Quintilia feels less
Sorrow from dying young
Than pleasure in your love.

101

I've made my way through many foreign tribes
And over many seas,
Now, brother, I have come
To these sad rites, to bring you, finally,
Your funeral gift, and speak
In vain, to the still dust
Since fate has taken your real self away,
O my poor brother, seized
Unworthily from me.
But never mind that now; accept these sad
Offerings for your grave,
Wet with a brother's tears
And offered in our fathers' ancient way,
And so, my brother, hail
Forever, and farewell.

LUCRETIUS

We have little reliable information about the life of Titus Lucretius Carus. St. Jerome tells us that he went insane as the result of a love-potion, wrote the *De Rerum Natura* in the lucid periods between attacks of madness, and died a suicide, but this account is probably as dubious as it is intriguing. It seems likely that St. Jerome, like other fathers of the early church, considered Lucretius, as an Epicurean philosopher, to be a vicious and dangerous enemy of religion. Even if Jerome's source for this biographical note was a pagan Roman writer, there is a likelihood there, too, of malicious falsification. Because Epicureans preached the private life and the rejection of the traditional Roman value of service to country, they found themselves disliked by state as well as church: One way or another, Epicureans were generally considered a subversive group, supercilious, clannish, and peculiar.

We do know that Lucretius lived from about 99 to 55 B.C., and that the orator and statesman Marcus Tullius Cicero read, praised, and perhaps edited his book in 54 B.C., although Cicero was not sympathetic to the Epicurean philosophy. The Lucretian family was well known and aristocratic, but we do not know if Lucretius was a member of it.

We have more facts about Epicurus, the founder of the school of philosophy to which Lucretius adhered. Epicurus was an Athenian (342–271 B.C.); in 306, he founded his school (which admitted women and slaves as well as freemen) in a garden at Athens. He was not only an important philosopher but also, apparently, an inspiring leader whose disciples felt for him a reverence bordering on worship. Epicurus felt that human happiness was and should be based on *hedone*—pleasure. This one word led and still leads to much misunderstanding and to much of the bad name Epicureans have always received from the naïve public. Both Epicurus and Lucretius make it quite clear that by pleasure they do not mean drunkenness, gluttony, and orgies; pleasure for an Epicurean can be maximized only by minimizing pain. Drunkenness, gluttony, and orgies lead to more pain than pleasure, as do the love of money and the pursuit of power. There is pleasure in friendship and in the simple gratification of bodily needs, and in the activities of philosophy. Philosophy (which includes science for the Epicureans as for most ancient philosophical schools) is particularly useful because it can help to eliminate one of the chief sources of pain in human life, fear.

There are two principal fears that disturb the minds of men, the fear of death and the fear of the gods. Both of these fears are irrational and can be dispelled by an understanding of the way the world really works. When we realize that the soul is mortal and purely physical, we will understand that there can be no pain, suffering, or sense of deprivation after death; therefore "Death is nothing to us" (*De Rerum Natura* 3.830). As for the fear of the gods, this arises because a) men think the gods cause the startling phenomena of nature, like lightning and earthquakes and disease, and b) men imagine that the gods regularly interfere with human affairs, rewarding prayer and punishing impiety. Neither of these is the case. When we come to a scientific understanding of the world, based on the materialistic system of atoms (adopted from Democritus), we no longer fear Zeus in the thunderbolt, and we no longer need to worry about appeasing the gods. There *are* gods—Epicurus was not an atheist—but they did not create the world, and they never interfere with it; we may contemplate their perfection and tranquillity if we like, but they won't be offended if we neglect them utterly.

Lucretius accepted the Epicurean system wholeheartedly, and set forth that system in a long poem, the *De Rerum Natura* ("On the Nature of Things"). The Greek prose of Epicurus (what we have left of it) is often unclear and ungraceful; the Latin poetry of Lucretius is lush, dramatic, mellifluous, and often moving. He concentrates on Epicurean physics, with only passing references to ethics, metaphysics, epistemology, and theology, but even the driest portions of this often complicated subject are enlivened by charming examples and proofs from daily life, and by artful imagery. The quality of the contents is uneven: Startlingly modern and correct observations will occur side by side with comical (and dogmatically stated) errors; the style, however, rarely falls below a high level of clarity and harmony. His words sound wonderful: it is almost impossible for a translator (for this translator, at least) to reproduce the beautiful combination of sound, rhythm, and meaning of lines like:

> processit longe flammantia moenia mundi
> or   non radii solis neque lucida tela diei
> or   placatumque nitet diffuso lumine caelum.

Lucretius may not have won many converts to Epicureanism with his work, but his style had great influence on later Roman poets, particularly Virgil and Ovid.

Book 1 of the *De Rerum Natura* sets forth the basic principles of the atomic theory; book 2 discusses motion, the combining of atoms, and various other characteristics of atoms; book 3 discusses the soul and argues against the fear of death; book 4 is concerned with sense perception and concludes with a delightful satirical attack on love; book 5 treats the origins of the earth and of life, and the evolution of man and society; book 6 discusses a number of puzzling natural phenomena, and concludes with a chilling description of the devastation of Athens by plague.

Out of this great banquet of wisdom and beauty, I regret that I can present only selections. If the reader is intrigued by these, he/she is warmly encouraged to go on to someone else's rendition of the whole work, or better yet, to enroll in a Latin course and look forward to the delight of reading the original.

DE RERUM NATURA

1.1–204

O mother of Aeneas' sons, O pleasure
Of men and gods, life-giving Venus, you
Who populate, beneath the gliding signs
Of heaven, all the navigable sea
And fill with life the harvest-bearing lands,
Through you each kind of creature is conceived
5 And rises up to see the light of day.
You, goddess, it is you who drive away
The winds; the clouds of heaven fly from you
And your approach; for you ingenious Earth
Sends up sweet-smelling flowers, and for you
The waves of Ocean smile while, pacified,
The heavens sparkle with far-spreading light.

10 As soon as spring unveils her morning face
The West Wind, fructifying, freed from prison
Blows strongly, and the birds of heaven first
Proclaim you, goddess, and reveal your strength,
As battering their hearts you enter in.
Then the wild beasts and placid cattle bound
Over the fertile pastures, and they swim
15 Across the hurrying streams; caught by your charm
Each follows hotly anywhere you lead.
Yes, over seas and hills and savage rivers
And leafy homes of birds, and grassy fields,
You hurl enchanting love into the hearts
Of every creature, and you make each one
20 Lustfully long to propagate his kind.

The Nature of Things is ruled by you alone;
And since without you nothing can be born
Into the shining coasts of light, nor be
Happy or lovable, I long for you
25 To be my ally, as I try to write
These verses about Nature, for my friend
Memmius, whom you, goddess, doubtless want[1]

---

1. Memmius—Gaius Memmius, a Roman politician of rather dubious and un-Epicurean character, to whom the work is dedicated. He ran for consul in 54 B.C. but was convicted of bribing voters and went into exile.

To shine at all times, and in everything.
Therefore, O goddess, give your lasting charm
To what I say, and meanwhile lay to rest
30 On sea and land the savage works of war.
For you alone can help us mortal men
With tranquil peace, since Mars, mighty-in-arms,
Rules the wild works of war; and you are she
Upon whose breast he often throws himself,
The conqueror conquered by the eternal wound
35 Of love; his graceful neck thrown back, he stares
Gasping, at you, and feeds his greedy eyes
With love, and hangs his breath upon your lips.
Encircle him, great lady, as he lies
Beneath your holy body; with those lips
40 Pour liquid language, begging peace for Rome.

In this uneven time of Rome's distress
I cannot study with a level head
Nor can a nobleman like Memmius
Desert the common welfare in such times.
Peace is your gift; the nature of the gods
45 Is wholly satisfied with perfect peace
Enjoyed forever, far removed from men.
Free from all sorrow, free from danger, strong
In riches of their own, the gods have need
Of nothing we can give; they are not pleased
By our good deeds, nor are they touched by rage.

50 Now, Memmius, hear me with open ears
And turn your sharpest thoughts, removed from care,
To true philosophy; do not disdain
My gifts, composed laboriously for you,
Before you understand them. I propose
To tell you of the highest laws of heaven
And of the gods, and will reveal to you
55 *Primordia*—"first-principles"; from these
All things are made by Nature, and with these
She nourishes and makes things grow; again,
All things, at death, dissolve back into these.
In our discussions, too, we sometimes say
"Matter" instead, "begetting-bodies," "seeds,"
60 Or we may say "first-bodies," since from them
As first beginnings all things have their cause.

When human life lay, hideous to see,
Prostrate on earth, crushed by religion's weight,
Religion showed her head, up in the sky,
65 And towered over men, with threatening looks,
Then first a mortal man, a Greek, was bold
Enough to raise his eyes to her, and stand
Opposing her; neither the myths of gods
Nor lightning stopped him, nor the heaven itself
With murmuring menace; all the more, his keen
70 Audacity of mind was sharpened, then,
So that he longed to be the first to break
The tightly fitting bolts on Nature's door.
The vigor of his mind won victory;
And, mentally, he traveled far beyond
The world's wide flaming walls, and visited
75 The boundless universe, from which he brings
His victor's prize to us: the facts which tell
What can arise and be, and what cannot,
And in what way each thing is limited
And where its deep-set boundary-mark is placed.
Religion now is trampled under foot,
And victory puts us in her place, in heaven!

80 I worry about this: that you may fear
We'll lead you into blasphemy, and start
You on the road to crime; quite the reverse!
Religion, oftener, has been the source
Of crime and blasphemy and wickedness.
As once at Aulis, when the altar of [2]
The maiden Trivia was given so foul
85 A stain by the blood of Iphianassa, shed
By statesmen, chosen men, the prime of Greece.
The victim's ribbon, round her girlish curls
Tumbled down both her cheeks; her parent stood
Before the altar, sad, while near to him
90 Servants concealed the knife; the citizens
Cried at the sight of her, as mute with fear
Humbly she sank, and knelt upon the earth.
He was the king, and she had been the first

2. Aulis—place where the Greek army gathered and were becalmed, before
going on to the Trojan War. *Trivia* is another name for the goddess Artemis
(Diana in Latin), who had stopped the winds. Iphianassa (also called
Iphigeneia) was the daughter of the Greek commander Agamemnon. He
sacrificed her to Artemis in order to get the winds blowing again.

To call him "father." This was no help to her,
95 Trembling, supported by the arms of men,
Led to the altar, not for the holy rites
And solemn ceremonies that precede
The raucous wedding song, but so that she
In age most ripe for marrying, most pure,
Might fall, impurely killed by her father's hand,
Sad sacrificial offering for the fleet
100 To make their sailing fair and fortunate.
Such wrongs Religion leads men to perform!

And you yourself, some time, will probably
Want to desert my school, when the Inspired
Have conquered you with terrifying words.
How many nightmares they can conjure up!
105 How thoroughly they can upset your way
Of life, and wreck your happiness with fear!
Of course: for if men knew that there would be
A definite conclusion to their pains,
They might be able to resist the priests
And face the threats of poets and of seers.
110 But as it is men do not have the way,
The power to resist: they are compelled
To fear eternal punishment in death.
They do not know the nature of the soul.
Is the soul born? Or, on the other hand,
Does it insinuate itself, at birth?
They do not know. When broken up by death,
Does it die with us? Or does it go to see
115 The shades of Orcus and the endless pits,
Or, by divine command, does it worm its way
Into some other beast, as Ennius sang?[3]
(Our Ennius was the first to bring a crown
Of everliving green down from the slope
Of lovely Helicon, to be called "great"
Throughout the tribes of Italy. And yet,
120 He also told us, in immortal verse,
That there exist regions of Acheron;[4]
Neither our souls nor bodies reach this place,
But certain pallid "likenesses" of us;

3. Ennius—Quintus Ennius (239–169 B.C.) was the first important Latin
poet. He wrote tragedies, comedies, satires, and an epic poem on the history
of Rome called the *Annales*. Only fragments of his works survive.
4. Acheron—the underworld.

From this place, Ennius tells us, came the shade
125 Of everliving Homer, and began
To weep salt tears, and teach the nature of things.)

Therefore: although we must explain the heavens,
And how the motions of the stars began,
And by what power all things are done on earth,
130 Still, before all, with logic and good sense
We must explore the nature of the soul
And of the mind, and of those nameless things
Which meet us in the tomb of sleep, or when
We are awake but ill, which terrify
Our minds, so that we seem to see and hear
Before us, face to face, those gone away
135 In death, whose bones lie in the arms of earth.
I know how hard it is, in Latin verse,
To shed light on the dark and difficult
Discoveries of the Greeks; the more so since
Often I must invent new terms, because
Latin is poor in words, and what I have
To say is very new. But still I am
140 Persuaded by your excellence, and by
The hoped-for joy of being your good friend,
To do whatever labor must be done,
And, like a watchman, keep awake throughout
The peaceful night, devising poetry
And phrases which will set before your mind
145 Bright lights, to help you see deep-hidden truths.

This terror, and these shadows of the mind
We must drive off, not with the Sun's bright rays,
Nor the bright shafts of day; we must dispel
This gloom with Nature's aspect and her Law.

Let us begin with this First Principle:
150 No thing is born from nothing, divinely, ever.
Terror grips all mankind, because they see
Many things happen in the earth and heaven
Whose cause they cannot know; therefore they think
Things can be made and done by heavenly Will.
155 And so, when we perceive that no thing can
Be made from nothing, we shall learn from this
More clearly, what we seek: how each thing can
Be made, that is created, and the way
Things can go on without the aid of gods.

If things could come from nothing, every class
Of thing could rise from anything, and none
160 Would need to have a seed. Men would be born
Out of the sea, and birds and the scaly tribe
Rise up out of the earth, and from the sky
Would burst forth flocks and cattle; every sort
Of beast would fill all types of habitat
Since parentage would make no difference.
165 A fruit tree would not always bear the same
Species of fruit, but orchards could exchange
Their roles, and any tree bear anything.
In fact, if every creature did not have
Its generative seed, how could there be
Known and consistent mothers for all things?
But, as it is, since creatures *do* possess
Their own distinctive seeds, from which they must
170 Be born and come forth to the coasts of light,
The matter and first-bodies of each thing
Must be inside the seed; because of this
All things can *not* arise from anything,
For each particular seed has, in itself,
Hidden inside, its own distinctive powers.

Why do we see the rose in spring, and grain
In summertime, and grapevines pouring forth
175 Their bounty under the coaxing of Autumnus,
If not that each created thing appears
At its appropriate season, when its seeds
Have flowed together, and the time is right,
And, full of life, the earth can safely bring
Her tender creatures into the coasts of light?

180 If things were born from nothing, suddenly
They might burst forth at hostile times of year
After no fixed gestation period,
Because, you see, they would not come from seeds
Which could be stopped from generation, when
The season is unfavorable. Again,
If things could grow from nothing, we would need
185 No time for growth, in which more seeds collect,
But suddenly, small babies would become
Young men, and full grown trees leap from the ground.
But clearly nothing of the sort occurs.
Each thing increases, rightly, by degrees,
From its own proper seed, and in its growth

190 Preserves its type; so you may see all things
    Grow and are nourished by appropriate
    Material. And now consider this:
    Without a rainy season every year
    The earth could not bring forth her jolly fruits,
    Nor, without food, could any living thing
195 Preserve its kind or keep its life. And so
    Isn't it reasonable to conclude
    That many things have tiny elements
    In common, just as different words may have
    Letters the same? And equally, we must
    Reject the notion that things can exist
    Without first-bodies. Lastly, why could not
    Nature produce men of such size that they
200 Could wade across the sea in giant steps,
    Move aside mountains with their monstrous hands,
    And outlive many centuries of life?
    These things do not occur, because the stuff
    Provided for begetting things is fixed;
    Its nature limits what things can arise.

1.248–64

    No thing turns into nothing, but all things
    Turn back at death into their natural seeds.
250 The rains may perish when the father sky
    Pours them into the lap of mother earth,
    But shining grain grows up to take their place;
    Tree branches bloom and grow and swell with fruit;
    And from this grain and fruit the race of men
255 And beasts is fed, and we see fertile towns
    Blossom with children, and the leafy woods
    Sing with the sound of baby birds, and cows
    Lay down the tiring burden of their bodies
    Throughout the fertile pastures; shining milk
    Flows from their swollen udders, while the calves,
260 Their young brains tipsy from the heady drink,
    Lustfully leap on shaky legs, and play
    Over the tender grass. Therefore, no thing
    Which is, can ever perish totally,
    Since Nature makes one thing out of another,
    And lets no thing be born unless she is
    Helped at its birth by the death of something else.

1.295–321

295   Therefore I say again and again: the wind
     Is *physical*, has body, though we cannot
     See it, for in its habits and results,
     It acts just like a swiftly-flowing stream,
     Which we can clearly see is physical.
     We feel the various smells of things, although
     We never see them coming to our nose,
300   We cannot see the heat, nor can we grasp
     Cold with our eyes, nor do we look at voices.
     But all these things must be made up of bodies
     Since they can move our senses: only bodies
     (And nothing else) can touch and can be touched.
305   Clothes hanging on wave-shattered shores grow wet;
     The same spread in the sun grow dry again.
     No one can see the water settling in,
     Nor, when it flees the heat, can it be seen.
     The water must be broken up so fine
310   That no one can observe its particles.
     Then too, with many cycles of the sun's
     Return, a finger ring wears thin inside
     And dripping water hollows out a stone;
     Subtly the iron plowshare in the furrow
315   Grows smaller; we can see on cobbled streets
     The pavement worn where many feet have walked.
     Bronze statues next to doors can be observed
     With their right hands rubbed thin by passersby
     Greeting them with a touch as they go through.
320   We see these things diminished, through long wear,
     But Nature jealously forbids our seeing
     Which bodies leave at any given time.

1.329–67

     Matter is not packed tightly in all things,
330   For there is *void* in objects. This will be
     Useful in many ways for you to know;
     This knowledge will correct your wandering
     Uncertainty, your constant questioning
     About the "sum of things," your lack of faith.
     So, there is space: untouchable and void
335   And empty. If there were not such a thing,

Nothing could move. The duty of matter is
To stand and block the way, and this is always
Present in every thing. Therefore without
Some space, no thing could ever move, since nothing
340 Would yield a place to it. But now, we see
Through seas and lands and through the heights of heaven,
Before our eyes, a multitude of motions
Of many various types, which could not be
If void were lacking, not so much because
Bodies would be deprived of restless movement,
But because motion could never start, since matter
345 Tight-packed, would fill the whole still universe.
Moreover, there are objects which appear
Solid, but from the following examples
You'll learn that they are porous: liquid moisture
Seeps through the walls of caves, and all the rocks
Weep copious teardrops; food is dissipated
350 Throughout the bodies of all living things;
Trees grow and in due season push out fruits
Abundantly, because their food is spread
Throughout their bodies, from the lowest roots
Up through their trunks and branches; voices find
Their way through walls, and fly through locked house-doors;
355 And stiffening cold goes through us to the bone.
You'd never see this happen if there were
No void in objects, through which things can pass.
And finally, why do we see one thing
Outweigh another thing of equal size?
360 If the amount of matter is the same
In a ball of wool as in a ball of lead,
Their weights should be the same, since matter's job
Is to press down, in everything, but void
By nature has no weight; so if one thing
Is larger than a second, but still weighs
The same, the first declares itself to have
365 More space inside it; heavier things reveal
They have more body in them, and less void.

1.498–519

True reason and the nature of things compel
Us to proceed: come now, and I'll explain
In several verses, that there do exist

500 Some things with solid and eternal bodies:
There are, we teach, "primordia," the seeds
Of things, from which the universe is made.
Now since we know there are two unlike kinds
Of nature, totally different from each other,
505 Matter and Space, in which all things go on,
Each one, then, must exist pure by itself.
For where a space is empty, which we call
"Void," there can be no matter, and where matter
Stands firm, there cannot be an empty space.
510 First-bodies, then, are solid, without void.
Now, since created objects do have space
Within, that space must be enclosed by matter.
True reason cannot find a thing which hides
Void in its body, if that thing does not
515 Hold in that void with solid material.
Matter, therefore, with solid body, is
Eternal, while all other things dissolve.

1.538–50

If, then, first-bodies are, as I have taught,
Solid, and have no void within, they must
540 Be everlasting. For if they were not,
By now the universe would have died down to nothing
And what we see before us would have been
Reborn from nothing—but I proved, above,
That *nothing* can be born from nothing, and
What is created cannot be called back
To nothing again. Therefore, *primordia*
595 Must have immortal bodies, into which
All things dissolve at their last hour, and these
Supply material for new-made things.
First-bodies have a solid simpleness;
For in no other way could they survive
550 Through infinite ages and make all things new.

1.921–50

Now, learn the rest, and hear a clearer song.
I'm not deceived; I know well how obscure
My subject is, but hope of fame has struck

My heart with a pointed thyrsus, and has driven[5]
Sweet love of the Muses into my breast, so now
925 Inspired, with racing mind, I wander over
The Muses' pathless mountains, in those places
Where no one's foot has walked. It is my pleasure
To visit virgin fountains and to drink,
And pleasure to pick fresh flowers, hoping they
Will make a remarkable garland for my head,
930 Of blossoms never used before by one
The Muses crowned. I teach important things
And try to break Religion's knotted bonds
Which tie the mind. I take dark thoughts and make
Them into lucid songs, well flavored with
935 Poetic beauty. Here is my reasoning:
When doctors give small children nauseous wormwood
First they moisten the edges of the cup
With the sweet taste of liquid yellow honey,
To play upon the child's young innocence
940 As far as the lips, at least; meanwhile, the child,
Deceived but not betrayed, drinks down the bitter
Wormwood, and in this way grows well and strong;
So now, because our doctrine seems to many
(Who have not learned it) to be rather hard
945 And it repels the masses, I have tried
To set it out in sweet-voiced poetry
And flavor it with honey from the Muses,
In hopes that by this method I might keep
Your mind attentive to my song, until
You grasp the nature of the universe
950 And see the reasons why it has this form.

2.1–62

How sweet it is to view, from land, great waves
Whipped by the whirling winds, and see the sailors
Laboring hard—not that it is a pleasure
To see another suffer—but to perceive
Evils that do not trouble us is sweet;
5 And it is sweet from a safe range to view
A battlefield, and see the troops drawn up,
But nothing is so happy as to stand

5. Thyrsus—a pointed staff, sort of a magic wand, carried by the followers of
Bacchus.

On the high ground, well fortified, serene,
Raised up by wise men's doctrines, and to look
Down on the others, see them wandering,
10 Aimlessly searching for a way of life,
Competing with their talents, fighting for
Social position, striving night and day
With monstrous struggling, to scale the height
Of money, and to dominate all things.

O pitiful minds of men! O blinded souls!
15 In what dark shadows, what great fancied risks
Our little life is wasted! Don't you see
That nature howls for nothing more than this:
A body lacking pain, a mind removed
From fear and worry, free for happiness?

20 We see our bodily nature needs few things:
Those which can take away the body's pains,
And in so doing, furnish us delights,
Often, most pleasant ones. But Nature herself
Does not feel deprivation, if no golden
Statues of youths, throughout the mansion, stand
25 With fiery torches in their hands, to give
Light to our nightly banqueting, nor does
The house blaze bright with silverplate, or shine
With gold, nor do the inlaid, gilded beams
Cry back the music of a harp. But we
Can satisfy our bodies happily
At small expense: we lounge on the soft grass
30 Among our friends, stretched out beside a stream
Under a tall tree's branches, when the weather
Smiles, and the season sprinkles the grass with flowers.

Hot fevers do not leave the body quicker
35 If you lie tossing on a purple quilt
Among brocaded spreads, than if you have
Plebeian covers over you. Therefore,
Since treasures bring no profit to the body,
Nor does high birth or the glory of a kingdom,
They also cannot ease a troubled mind.
40 Even if you have legions, and can watch
Them seething on the Campus, in a show[6]

6. Campus—the Campus Martius ("Field of Mars"), a park and parade-ground in Rome.

Of martial arts, well armed and spirited,
Flanked by reserves and powerful cavalry,
Can these things frighten Religion, so she'll run
45　In terror from your mind? Or scare your fears
Of Death, so they'll depart, and leave your breast
Free and relieved of worry? No; we see
The thought is laughable, ridiculous.
In fact, the fears of men, their dogged worries
Do not fear savage weapons or the crash
50　Of arms, but brashly stride about among
Kings and the powerful—they have no awe
Of blazing gold or splendid purple clothes.
Why doubt it? Power to free oneself from fear
Belongs to Reason alone, especially
Since all our life is labor in the dark.

55　As children tremble, and fear everything
They see in the blind shadows, so we too
In daylight are afraid, of nothing but
The sorts of things that children fear at night
When, shuddering, they think their dreams are real.
This terror and these shadows of the mind
We must drive off, not with the sun's bright rays
60　Nor the bright shafts of day; we must dispel
This gloom with Nature's aspect and her law.

3.830–58

830　Death, then, is nothing to us; it does not touch us
A bit, because we know the soul is mortal.
Just as we felt no anguish, long ago,
When Carthage came attacking on all sides,[7]
When the world trembled, shivering beneath
835　The deep sky borders, struck by the rattling clash
Of war, and no one knew to which side luck
Would fall to rule mankind and earth and sea,
Thus, when we are no more, when there has been
A splitting of soul and body, out of which
840　Our selves were put together, clearly then

7. Carthage—the Punic Wars (264–241, 218–201, 149–146 B.C.) between
Rome and the Punic (Carthaginian) Empire led to the establishment of
Rome's position as the dominant power in the world, and the complete de-
struction of Carthage.

No thing can touch us or can make us feel
When we are nothing—no, not even if
Earth be mixed up with sea, and sea with sky!
Even if power to feel remained in soul
Or spirit, after it is torn away
845 From body, this would not pertain to us,
Since *we* exist only when soul and body
Unite and join together in a self.
Even if Time should gather all our atoms
After our death and put them back together
Just as they are today, and once again
The light of life were given, even this
850 Would not affect us, once our consciousness
Was interrupted. Now, we are not touched
By any former selves which used to be,
Nor do we feel distress because of them.
When you consider all the boundless length
855 Of time which has passed by, and all the motions
Of matter every which way, you might find
It easy to imagine that our seeds
Have often been arranged as they are now
In times before; but nonetheless, we cannot
Grasp with our memories those former lives.

3.870–87

870 When you find a man indignant at the thought
That after death his body will decay
Or be consumed by flames or by the jaws
Of beasts, you may be sure that, even though
He *says* he knows no feelings will remain
After his death, his words do not ring true:
875 Somewhere inside, blind fears are jabbing him.
He doesn't really pay up what he promised;
He doesn't tear himself up by the roots
And expel himself from life; unconsciously
He makes some small part of himself survive.
When a living man supposes that his body
880 Will be torn up in death by birds or beasts
He's pitying himself, for he does not
Distinguish his dead body from himself
Nor separate himself from the cast-off corpse,
But sees it as himself, and "standing by,"
Adulterates it with his living feelings.

He who complains that he was created mortal
885 Does not perceive that after death no other
Self will survive to mourn his death, or stand
Weeping for him who lies in shreds or ashes.

3.894–901

"Now, now, no longer will your happy household
And splendid wife embrace you! Never again
895 Will your sweet children race to be the first
To grab a kiss from you, and touch your heart
With silent happiness! Now you have lost
The flowers of your success; now you will not
Stand guard over your family. You poor man"—
They say—"One loathsome day has wickedly
Snatched all the many prizes of your life!"
900 But here is what they fail to add: "No longer
Will you have any craving for these things."

3.912–51

It often happens when a party of men
Lounge at the table and the drinks go round,
With faces shadowed by their slipping wreaths,
They say, with passion, "We poor puppet-men
Have much too short a time for pleasure; soon
915 It will be gone, and never can come back!"
As if the awful thing about their death
Would be a parching thirst and burning dryness
Or any other craving! But in fact
No one feels need of self or life when his
920 Body and soul rest equally in sleep;
At such times we could go on sleeping always
And never feel the lack of our waking selves.
And yet in sleep the atoms of our souls
Cannot be wandering too far from our senses,
925 For men who are shaken wake immediately
And gather themselves together. Therefore, we
Should think of death as an even lesser thing
Than sleep—if something can be "less" which we
Can see is nothing—for with death, the crowd
Of atoms is more disturbed, and no one wakes
930 When once his life has stopped and he grows cold.

Suppose that suddenly, the Nature of Things
Should find a voice, accusing one of us:
"What is so terribly the matter, mortal,
That you give in to whining lamentation?
Why all this grief and groaning over death?
935 If life before now has been good to you
So that your pleasures have not all been lost
As if they ran together through a sieve
And drained away to nothing, why not take
Your leave, you silly man, like a guest who's had
His fill of life, and cheerfully lie down
940 To your untroubled sleep? But if the fruits
Of life have slipped away and died to you,
And living is repulsive, why be eager
For more of it when this too will turn out
Badly, and nothing pleasant will remain?
Isn't it better to be finished with
Your life and struggle? *I* cannot devise
945 Or find a thing to please a man like you:
All things remain the same. You have a body
Not withered yet, by years, nor are your limbs
Worn out and slow, but still, no new delight
Remains for you, not even if you live
Through many generations, no, not even
If you should never die"—what can we answer,
950 Except that Nature pleads a lawful claim
And that her arguments are just and true?

3.964–76

Old things are always ousted and must yield
965 To new; each thing must be remade from others.
No man goes down to hell or to the black
Abyss of Tartarus: his atoms are[8]
Needed, so that the future generations
May grow—and when these too have lived their lives,
They'll follow you, and fall as you have fallen.
970 So it goes on forever: each thing born
From others; life is never owned outright
By anyone; we share its use as tenants.
Think of the ancient past, how many years
Of endless time went on before our birth—

8. Tartarus—still another name for the underworld.

To us, these all are nothing; and in these,
We see, as in a mirror held by Nature,
975 The time that waits for us beyond our death.
Is any fear apparent in that image?
Is any sorrow there? Isn't the picture
More tranquil than the most untroubled sleep?

4.1037–1134

This semen, as I said before, is stirred
In us, when first our limbs are strengthened by
Adulthood. Different causes stimulate
And stir up different things. In human beings,
Only the power of another human
1040 Can rouse the seed to burst forth from the body.
Jarred from its seats, it runs down through the limbs
And members of the body, and collects
In part of the groin, where instantly, it starts
To stimulate the genitals themselves.
1045 Excited, they begin to swell with seed,
And the wish forms to throw that semen out
To the place toward which the fatal lust is straining,
That body which has hurt the mind with love.
Men fall in the direction of their wounds
1050 And blood spurts toward the blow; a crimson stream
Falls on the enemy, if he is near;
In the same way, the man who is wounded by
The weapons of Venus—whether the one who threw
The dart was a boy with girlish body, or
A woman, throwing passion's javelins
1055 From every part—still strains toward those parts which
Have struck him, and he longs to come together
And cast the liquid from his body to
The body of his lover; his desire
Though silent, tells him pleasure is to come.

Such is our goddess Venus, and from this
Desire—*cupido*—"Cupid" comes, and gives
His name to love. From this desire, we first
Feel the sweet drops of Venus' honey seep
1060 Into our hearts, and then her chilling pains.
For even if your loved one is away,
Her image stays with you; her lovely name

Keeps coming to your ears. You should avoid
Those images, and chase away the food
Which love is fattened on! Direct your mind
1065 To other objects; cast your gathered liquid
Into some other body. If you try
To save it, fixed upon one love alone,
What you will save is trouble for yourself
And certain pain. An ulcer will survive;
Your tender care will make it chronic; your
Fever will blaze up higher every day,
Your suffering grow heavy, if you don't
1070 Lance that first sore with newer blows and heal
Your wounds, while they are fresh, by wallowing
In the lap of a lolling trollop, or, if you[9]
Are able, turn your mind to other things.
Avoid love, you do not have to miss
The fruits of Venus; rather, you consume
Goods that are free from penalty. In fact
1075 Your pleasure, if you're sane and cool, is purer
Than that of wretched lovers. Even when
They reach the very moment of possession
Their lovers' ardor tosses on a sea
Of restless indecisiveness, unsure
What first to seize on with their eyes and hands.
The things they sought, they crush, inflicting pain
1080 Upon the body; teeth smash into lips;
Kisses are made to hurt. Their pleasure is
Impure, confused by love; beneath the surface
Are spurs, which jab and lead them to attack
That thing which caused the germination of
Their madness. But indulgent Venus treats
These love attacks as harmless, and seductive
1085 Mixed pleasure curbs the biting teeth. For there
Is hope, that in the same place where the fire
Arose, these flames can be extinguished by
That very body. Nature, however, wholly
Forbids it. Love is unique in this: the more
1090 We get, the brighter glows the fatal spark
Of longing in us. Food and drink are taken
Into our bodies, fill up certain parts,
And satisfy our hunger and our thirst.

9. "Wallowing in the lap of a lolling trollop"—Lucretius's phrase, *vulgivaga-
que vagus Venere*, is no less lushly alliterative.

But from a human's face and lovely color
Our bodies can get nothing but the flimsy
1095 Pictures of satisfaction, snatched from the air
By wretched hope. As a thirsty, sleeping man
Who wants to drink, and water is not given
To quench his burning anguish, grasps at pictures
Of liquids in his dream, and struggles in vain
1100 In the middle of a flooding river, still
Thirsty—so, in passion, Venus mocks
Lovers with pictures; they cannot be sated
By looking, even face to face, nor can
Their hands, which wander aimlessly all over
The body, rub off anything at all
From the soft limbs. Then, when the limbs are locked
1105 Together, and they pick the flower of youth,
And when their bodies speak of pleasure to come,
And Venus is at work to sow the woman's
Fertile field, they squeeze their eager bodies
Together, and they mingle their saliva,
and, pressing teeth on lips, they breathe each other's
1110 Breath—to no avail, since they cannot
Rub off a thing, nor penetrate the whole
Body, nor merge one body in the other.
It sometimes seems that this is what they want
and struggle for, so eagerly they stay
Glued in the bonds of Venus, while their limbs
Are broken down and melted by the force
1115 Of ecstasy. At last, when the collected
Lust bursts out of the genitals, there is
A pause in the violent burning, for a while.
Then the disease returns; the insanity
Comes back; they look for what they want, some means
To cure their pain, but no—in ignorance
1120 They sicken, wasted by internal wounds.
Then, too, the lover, worn out by the work
Of love, grows weak, and wastes his youth, subdued
By another's nod; his duties go undone;
His reputation staggers and takes sick,
His money melts away, turns into perfumes
From Babylon, while pretty slippers, made
1125 In Sicyon, smile on his mistress' feet.
Oh, yes. Enormous emeralds give off
Green sparkles, set in gold; the ocean-purple
Dress is worn thin by constant lovers' struggles,
And sponges up the sweat that Venus brings.

The wealth his father earned goes into ribbons
1130 And head-scarves, or a cloak, or foreign fabrics.
A banquet is prepared, with tasteful linens,
Fine food, drinks, gambling, perfumes, garlands, crowns—
In vain. For in the middle of the fountain
Of pleasure bubbles up a bitter taste
1134 To bring him pain among the very flowers.

4.1155–70

1155 The foulest, ugliest women can be seen
To be adored, and held in highest honor.
So one man laughs at another, and advises
Him to propitiate Venus, since he is
Afflicted with a foul infatuation;
Meanwhile he doesn't see that his is worse.
1160 The sallow girl is "honey-gold," the dirty
And smelly one is "natural," the one
Whose eyes are muddy is "grey-eyed Athena,"
The hard and stringy athlete's "a gazelle,"
The midget is "pure sparkle," "one of the Graces,"
The hulking giant's "dignified," "a marvel,"
The stammerer has "such a charming lisp,"
1165 The mute is "modest," the obnoxious big mouth
Is "brilliant," while the one who's almost starved
To death is "such a slender little dear,"
And "delicate" is what that girl is called
Whose cough has almost killed her, but the fat
And busty one is "Ceres, just the way
She looked when nursing Bacchus," and the pug-nosed
Is called a "Satyress" or "girl Silenus";
The girl with fleshy lips is "one big kiss."
1170 In sum, the list is much too long to finish.

POETS OF THE

AUGUSTAN
AGE

VIRGIL

P. Vergilius Maro was born in 70 B.C., near present-day Mantua, which was then in the province of Gaul. His family was lower-class but had Roman citizenship; Virgil himself was said to look like a hick. He was almost pathologically shy, virginal, and reclusive and had some problem with speaking, so it is not surprising that, although trained for a legal career, he gave up the law after one public performance. From about 43 to 37 B.C., he composed the ten pastoral poems known as the *Eclogues* ("Selections") or *Bucolics* ("Cowherd Songs"). At some point during or just after he wrote these, his life entered a new phase. He won the attention and support of Octavian (who was to become Augustus, the first emperor), and became a protégé of Octavian's rich friend Maecenas, the famous literary patron. He made friends with the poet Horace, whom he introduced to Maecenas. He moved to Naples, where he spent the next seven years writing the four books of *Georgics* ("Farming"). Virgil was a slow, careful writer; for the rest of his life (the next eleven years) he worked on his epic poem, the *Aeneid*, which he never finished to his own satisfaction. On a trip to Greece in 19 B.C., he became ill, and just after reaching Italy again, he died. His last wish was that the *Aeneid* be destroyed, but Augustus saved the poem. The poet was buried in Naples.

The *Aeneid*, of course, is Virgil's famous work, the work that has been praised, imitated, and even read from his day to the present. But it was *Eclogues* 4, with its apparent prophecy of the birth of Christ, that made Virgil and all his works acceptable to the doctrinaire eyes of the Middle Ages, when the beauty and cleverness of most Greek and Roman "pagans" were regarded as dangerously seductive. (Incidentally, scholars are still arguing about who the baby is in *Eclogues* 4. There were several prominent pregnant ladies in Rome at the time, and Virgil may have been hedging his bets, deliberately speaking vaguely in order to compliment several powers at the same time.) At any rate the *Aeneid* still remains popular, although at the moment many critics see less noble patriotism and more rueful irony in the poem than has been seen in the past. And the *Eclogues* are much studied, too, by historians looking for political allusions and by literary critics uncovering complicated levels of meaning. Just as a theologian (for example) may find religious significance in everything he or she reads and sees, and a pathologist, say, may be constantly startled by evidences of disease everywhere, and an accountant, perhaps, may sometimes feel that the world is made up of nothing but numbers, just so there is a tendency among literary critics to find that all works are, at bottom, about literary criticism and all poems really about poetry. The *Eclogues* are particularly subject to this approach, perhaps because, to some extent, they really *are* poems about poems.

Virgil is among Roman poets the one most influenced by his Greek predecessors. The chief source of the *Aeneid* is Homer; the chief source of the *Eclogues* is Theocritus; the *Georgics* are modeled chiefly on the work of Hesiod. Homer, of course, was one of the greatest poets of all time; Theocritus, too, is a very fine poet. Virgil did not surpass either of these models. But the *Georgics* is a wonderful poem, an Italian, not a Greek, poem quite different from and far superior to Hesiod's *Works and Days*. To my mind, it is Virgil's masterpiece. (I must say that I share this opinion with Dryden, and with few others.) The two great didactic poems of Latin literature (the *Georgics* and Lucretius's *De Rerum Natura*) surely have two of the most unpromising subjects possible for poetry: agriculture and physics. We would probably have to look to the modern age of technology (to an epic-length "Manual of Air Conditioning," say, or an "Encomium on the Wankel Rotary Engine") to find anything so devoid of conventional "inspiration." But both poets succeed brilliantly at their difficult jobs; they digress and decorate, to be sure, but they do not belittle their subjects. They are serious; they do not act bored, and consequently, they are seldom boring—never as boring as, for example, Ovid gets toward the end of the *Metamorphoses*, where he has the advantage of stories that are either erotic or violent or (usually) both.

And in the *Georgics* Virgil set himself a doubly difficult task. He chose to glorify farming—with the approval of Augustus, whose reforms included a campaign to get the welfare poor out of the city and back to the farms—and he chose to glorify it not by romanticizing the beauties of nature or the relaxed life of the farmer but by emphasizing the *difficulty* of farming. Apparently, the Roman civil war had disturbed the poet deeply, had depressed him about human nature. And so he determined to make agriculture seem like the moral equivalent of war, like a challenging, adventurous battle with Nature, worthy to engage not the pleasure-loving part of people but their hostile, aggressive side. So it is a tough, realistic poem, a passionately thoughtful one, and, because of his exquisitely polished, sweet-sounding Latin, a beautiful one. You couldn't really operate a farm using the *Georgics* as a handbook. But reading it might make you *want* to operate one, something that a work like Cato's *De Agri Cultura* (which actually tells you where to buy your millstone) could never do.

It is easy to dismiss Virgil as excessively pure and respectable, and to sneer at him for being too much the fair-haired boy of the Augustan establishment. But he is too good a poet to reject lightly. He is best, of course, in his own lovely Latin. But even in translation, it may be hoped that some echoes of his grave, melancholy music still remain.

ECLOGUES

2

The shepherd Corydon loved his master's lover,
Charming Alexis, but he hoped in vain.
Day after day he walked among the beeches
And shadowed by their cover,
Alone, made awkward speeches,
The woods and mountains heard the fool complain:

"Cruel Alexis, pity my desire!
Do you scorn my singing? Must I die in pain?
The cows are looking for a shady place
Lizards are lying hidden in the briar
Now Thestylis grinds pungent herbs together,
Wild thyme and garlic for the men worn out
From reaping in this weather,
But what reward do I get when I trace
Your footsteps in this sun? I get the rattle
Of crickets on the vine.
Though Amaryllis nagged and used to pout,
Wasn't her anger better than this lack?
Menalcas, almost black,
Was kinder. Fair-haired boy, don't trust to your
Complexion: hyacinths, though dark, are chosen,
White privet falls.
                    "Despising me, you will
Not ask about me, learn that I am rich
In snowy milk and cattle:
A thousand lambs upon that ridge are mine,
In summertime my milk runs fresh and pure,
As when the ground is frozen,
I call my flock with songs like those in which
The Theban Amphion charmed the Attic hill.[1]
I'm not so hideous, either; when the sea
Stood calm the other day I saw my face.
If mirrors cannot lie, I need not fear
Daphnis himself.
                    "O, if you'd live with me!
We'd share my wretched fields and hut, and chase

1. Amphion—a legendary musician. He built a wall around the city of Thebes by using the magical power of his lyre to move the rocks.

The kids together with a supple stick,
Or stalk the deer,
You'll rival Pan: I'll teach you how to sing
—Our Pan, the shepherd's friend, first taught the trick
Of joining reeds with wax; he guards our sheep—
It should not hurt your lip to blow sweet tones
(Amyntas would have *died* to learn the art.)
Then, if you come, I'll bring
A seven-stalk hemlock pipe which you may use,
A gift Damoetas gave to me to keep
And said 'Now you're the second man it owns.'
(Silly, jealous Amyntas ate his heart.)
There are two fawns I rescued in a steep
Ravine just lately, now my milking ewes
Suckle them twice a day,
Their coats are flecked with white,
They are your fawns, Alexis, if you choose.
Thestylis covets them; she'll get them, too,
Since all my gifts are rubbish in your sight.
Come, charming child! The Nymphs are courting you,
Their brimming baskets hold
Lilies, And look, the Naiad brings a spray,
Pale violets and giant poppies twined
With yellow jonquils, sweetly smelling dill,
Wild cinnamon and other herbs combined,
A picture painted brightly
With hyacinth and yellow marigold.
And I myself will gather peaches, lightly
Dusted with snowy down, and I will pick
Chestnuts, which Amaryllis used to favor,
And waxy plums (for this tree also will
Be honored), next I'll put some myrtle in
With laurel, blended for sweet mingling savor.
O Corydon, you hick.
Alexis doesn't care for gifts at all
And if he did, Iollas still would win.
What was I thinking of?
To let the Southwind rage among my flowers
And boars tramp through my once-clear waterfall?
Idiot, why do you run? Immortal powers
Live in the woods, and Paris herded sheep.
Let Pallas keep the towers[2]

2. Pallas—Pallas Athene (Lat. Minerva), who was goddess of cities as well as
wisdom.

That she has built; the woods are what I treasure.
As, with a savage love
The lioness hunts the wolf, who hunts the kid,
The lusting kid runs after flowering heath,
I follow you, for each obeys his pleasure
Whatever it may bid.
Look! The bullocks are dragging home the plow
Unhitched, while underneath
The falling sun the shadows rise more deep:
Yet love is torturing me even now.
O Corydon, what sickness holds your mind!
Among the leafy elms all day you leave
Your vines half-pruned; get busy now and weave
Rushes or twigs, or do *some* useful thing;
If this Alexis spurns you, you will find
Another one, who wants to hear you sing."

4

Sicilian Muses, help me now to sing[3]
A serious song. Low-growing shrubs and trees
Do not please all; if woods are in my verse,
Let them be woods a consul might approve.

Now comes the last age of the Sibyl's book;[4]
The famous cycle of the centuries
Is born again: the Virgin will return[5]
And soon the reign of Saturn will come back[6]
And highest heaven send down a newborn race.
Your own Apollo rules on earth; therefore,
Look kindly, pure Lucina, on the boy[7]
Soon to be born, through whom the Iron Age
Will start to dwindle—under whom a race
Of Gold will rise up over all the world.
The glorious era will begin when you

3. Sicilian Muses—Virgil calls on the Muses of Sicily because Theocritus, his Greek predecessor in pastoral poetry, came from that island.
4. The Sibyl's book—Sibyls were ancient half-legendary prophetesses. There were several collections of Sibylline books in ancient Rome, written and forged at various times. Chiefly due to Virgil's *Eclogues* 4 (this poem) the Sibyl of Cumae was later regarded as having predicted the birth of Christ.
5. The Virgin—here, probably, Justice.
6. Saturn—king of the gods before Jupiter.
7. Lucina—goddess of childbirth.

Are consul, Pollio, and the great months[8]
Commence their march; with you as leader, any
Traces of our old guilt which still remain
Will vanish, freeing the earth from constant fear.
He will receive the life of a god, and see
Heroes and deities, and will be seen
By them, himself, and he will rule a world
Made peaceful by his father's excellence.

Your first small presents, child, the Earth, untilled,
Will bear profusely: ivy everywhere
Will twine with baccar, and acanthus thorns
Mingle with colocasia's smiling cups.
Spontaneously the goats will carry home
Udders brimful with milk; cows will not fear
Great lions, and your crib itself will sprout
Enticing flowers for your earliest toys.
The snake will die; deceptive poison plants
Will die; Assyrian balsam will spring up
In every garden. Then, when you begin
To read the hero legends, and to learn
About your father's exploits, and can tell
What honor is, the grassy plains will start
To yellow, gradually, with tender corn;
Wild brambles will grow red with hanging grapes;
Hard oak trees will perspire with dewy honey.
But still some traces of our ancient crime
Will linger, causing men to violate
With ships the sea nymphs' province, to constrict
Their towns with girdling walls, to stab the earth
With furrows. Once again a Tiphys will[9]
Arise, and guide another Argo, filled
With chosen champions; more wars will come;
And a great Achilles go once more to Troy.[10]

But when maturing years make you a man,
Even the merchant will give up the sea,
The pine will not become a trading ship,
For every land will furnish everything.

8. Pollio—G. Asinius Pollio, a friend of Virgil's, soldier, statesman, historian, and patron of the arts; he built the first public library in Rome. He was consul in 40 B.C.
9. Tiphys—pilot of the legendary ship *Argo*, which took Jason and the Argonauts in quest of the golden fleece.
10. Achilles—Greek hero of the Trojan War.

The soil will not endure the hoe, nor vines
The pruning hook; the vigorous plowman will
Release his oxen from their yokes; no dyes
Will teach bright-colored falsehood to pure wool:
The ram, in the meadow by himself, will blush
Sweet crimson murex-color, then will change[11]
His fleece to saffron, while, spontaneously,
Vermilion clothes the young lambs as they graze.

"Keep spinning, circle of years," the Fates cried out
Together, to their spindles, as they sang
The long-established power of Destiny.

Dear offspring of the gods, great progeny
Of Jove—the time will soon be here—approach
The height of glory; look upon this world
Swaying beneath its convex load: the lands,
The spreading seas, the deep expanse of sky,
See how all things rejoice in the coming age!
If only one last part of my long life
Still waits for me, and spirit enough to tell
Your story, then I'll conquer Orpheus [12]
In singing, though his mother was a Muse;
And Linus, too, although he was the son
Of fair Apollo; even Pan, if he
And I competed, with Arcadia
As judge, yes, even Pan would have to say
I won—with his Arcadia as judge.

Come, little boy, it's time to show you know
Your mother, with a smile: ten months have brought
Long weariness to her; come, little boy
Begin: no boy who cannot learn to smile
Will ever be invited out to dine
With gods, or share his bed with goddesses.

11. Murex—valuable dye, made from the seashell murex.
12. Orpheus, Linus—mythical great musicians.

GEORGICS

1.43–83

In the early spring, when the cold frosts dissolve
Upon the mountains, white-topped like old men,
The west wind starts to soften the crumbling clods;
Then let your oxen groan under the plow
And may your plowshare glitter, all its rust
Worn off in the hard furrows. Greedy prayers
Are answered by that soil which twice has seen
The sunshine, and two times has felt the cold;
That soil will burst your barns with boundless crops.
But first, before your steel has split the plain,
You must become acquainted with the ways
Of various regions: their prevailing winds,
Their climates, what each area will bear
And what it will refuse—this one is good
For wheat, while that is luckier for grapes;
Fruit trees grow better here, but there the grass
Springs up unbidden. Have you not observed
That Tmolus sends to us the pungent scents
Of saffron, India gives ivory,
The soft Sabaeans render frankincense,
The naked Chalybes dig iron, while
Pontus yields fetid castor oil, and last,
Epirus breeds the mares that win the palm
At Elis? Nature herself imposed these laws [13]
For fixed locations, and has made, with them,
An everlasting treaty, since that day
So long ago, on which Deucalion, first, [14]
Threw stones into the empty world—from which
Mankind arose, a hardened race. Therefore,
Now, in the year's first months, as soon as you can,
Let your strong oxen turn the fertile soil;
Then let the summer, with her ripening suns,
Bake all the clods, which lie exposed, to dust.
But if your soil is meager, it will be
Enough to toss it lightly, in the fall,

13. Elis—the Olympic games were held in Elis, on the Peloponnesus in Greece.
14. Deucalion—the Greek Noah; he and his wife Pyrrha survived the Great Flood.

In shallow furrows: with your richer soil
The danger is that grass will choke the crops;
Your poorer, sandy soil has more to fear
From loss of moisture. Fields that have been shorn
Should, every other season, have a rest
And lying fallow, harden into crust,
Or, when the season changes, you may sow
The yellow grain where formerly you raised
Prolific beans which rattled in their pods
Or tiny vetches, or a whispering
Forest of fragile reeds, the bitter stalks
Of lupines. For a crop of flax will burn
The soil, and oats will burn, and poppies, too,
Swimming in Lethean sleep, will burn your land,
But crop rotation will reduce your work,
Only, you must not be ashamed to soak
The dried-out soil with rotted, rich manure,
And scatter filthy ashes over all
Your tired fields. And so, the land finds rest
With alternating crops, and you will find
Earth left unplowed will show her gratitude.

1.118–46

Cattle and men have labored long, and turned
The earth unceasingly, but nonetheless
The unrelenting goose, Strymonian cranes
And bitter chicory all carry on
Their steady enmity, while lack of sun
Does damage to the crops. The Father himself
Wanted the way of farming to be hard;
He caused the earth to need the plowman's art
And sharpened mortal minds by giving men
Troubles, so that his kingdom should not doze
In senile stupor. No one, before Jove,
Had worked a farm; it was unlawful, then,
To set up boundary marks or to divide
The fields; men gathered food on common land
And Earth herself gave all things liberally,
Since no one forced her. Then He introduced
Black serpents, with their poison, and the wolf
To hunt for prey; he caused the sea to toss;
He knocked the honey out of the leaves, and hid
Fire; then he stopped the flowing of the streams

Of wine, to insure that Practice alone, and Thought,
Might hammer out the various techniques,
Discover grain in furrows, and strike out
The fire which is concealed in veins of flint.
Then first the rivers felt the weight of trees
Hollowed by men, and sailors learned to name
The stars: the Pleiades, the Hyades,
Lycaeon's brilliant Bear. Men learned to catch
Wild animals with traps, and birds with lime,
And to surround the meadows with their dogs.
One flogs the deepest rivers with his net;
Another drags his wet lines through the sea.
Then came hard iron, and the chattering saw—
Although at first men used a wedge to split
Timber—and all the various skills emerged.
For unrelenting Work conquered all things,
Work and the pushing Needs of poverty.

1.438–514

The Sun, too, when he rises and when he
Plunges himself into the waves, will give
You signs: the surest portents follow him
Either at dawn or when the stars arise.
If flickering spots darken the newborn dawn
And clouds obscure the sun, or if his light
Flees to the outer edges of his disc,
Expect some rainy weather: the South Wind
Is pushing in from sea and threatening
Your trees, your fields, your flocks. But if his rays
Pierce intermittently through heavy clouds
At dawn, or if Aurora rises pale[15]
Leaving Tithonus in their golden bed,
Look out! for then the vine leaves will provide
Little protection for your tender grapes
When quantities of dreadful hailstones leap
And rattle on the roof. This, too, you must
Remember: when the stages of his trip
Through heaven are complete, and he declines,
And we see different colors wandering
Across his face, a bluish tint forecasts

15. Aurora, Tithonus—Aurora was the goddess of Dawn. Tithonus was her
mortal lover, who couldn't die but kept on aging.

Rain, and a fiery one, East Winds. But if
His golden fire is mixed with darker spots
Then you will see all nature equally
Seething with wind and storm. On such a night
No one could force me to cast off my ropes
And leave the land behind, to sail the sea.
But if, when day returns, or when he hides
The day again, you see a shining sphere,
You need not fear the clouds, for you will learn
The woods are stirred only by fair North Winds.
In short, the Sun will tell you all these things:
What the late evening brings, what sort of wind
Pushes the peaceful clouds, or what the damp
South Wind is planning.
                              Who would dare to call
The Sun a liar? For he even warns,
Often, that unforeseen disasters are
Impending, and that treachery and plans
For war are swelling secretly. That time
When Caesar's light went out, the Sun revealed[16]
His pity for the Romans, for he veiled
His shining face in rusty-dark eclipse,
So that the sinful people were afraid
The night would last forever. At that time
The earth gave portents, also, and the sea,
And dogs howled evil luck and sinister
Birds gave a warning; often, we observed
Mount Aetna heaved, and from the Cyclopes'[17]
Burst-open furnaces, a wave of fire
Glowed in the fields, and balls of flame rolled down
With melted rocks. In Germany, the troops
Heard sounds of battle thundering in the sky,
And the Alps shook with tremors never felt
Before. The sound of a great voice was heard
By many, in the silent woods, and shapes
Of pallid ghosts appeared in darkest night;
And—horrible!—cattle spoke human words.
Streams stopped, the earth gaped open, and we saw
In shrines, the saddened ivory statues weep
And bronze ones burst into a sweat of rage.

16. Caesar's light—the assassination of Julius Caesar, 44 B.C.
17. Cyclopes—one-eyed giants; they run a blacksmith's shop under the vol-
canic Mt. Aetna.

The Eridanus, king of rivers, flowed [18]
Over his banks, with crazy eddying
And swept the woods away, over the fields,
Along with stalls and cattle. Constantly
The sacrificial victims' inner parts
Showed threatening fibers, and from drinking wells
The blood came bubbling up, while, through the night,
The tallest cities heard the echoing wail
Of wolves. No other age has ever heard
More thunder crash in cloudless skies, nor seen
Unlucky comets blaze so many times.
Then, once again, the fields of Philippi [19]
Saw Roman troops attacking Roman troops
With equal weapons, and the gods allowed
Emathia and Haemus' spreading farms
Twice to be fertilized with Roman blood.
No doubt the time will come when in that land
Some farmer, heaving earth with his curved plow
Will come upon a spear, half-eaten away
By scabby rust; his heavy hoe will strike
An empty helmet; he will wonder that
The shattered sepulcher yields such big bones.
Gods of our fathers, gods of our native soil!
Romulus, mother Vesta, you who guard
The Tuscan Tiber and the Palatine,
Do not forbid this one young man, at least, [20]
To help our fallen age! Have we not paid
Already, with our blood, the penalty
For that false oath sworn by the Trojan king? [21]
Already, Caesar, there is jealousy
In heaven's courts: they wonder why you care
For human triumphs, in a world where Right
And Wrong are so inverted, in a world
Filled with so many wars, so many forms
Of wickedness, no honor for the plow,
The farms neglected, with their masters gone,
And curved scythes melted into rigid swords.

18. Eridanus—the Po River.
19. Philippi—town in Macedonia, where Mark Antony defeated Cassius and Brutus, the assassins of Caesar, in the battle that ended the Roman Republic.
20. Young man—Augustus.
21. Trojan king—Laomedon, the father of Priam, who had the nerve to swindle first the gods Apollo and Poseidon, then the hero Hercules. The Trojans are regarded as the ancestors of the Romans; therefore Roman suffering could be seen as a punishment for Laomedon's tactless ways.

Here, Parthia, there Germany stirs up
New troubles, and the towns of Italy
Bear arms against each other, while their laws
Have broken down; the godless god of war
Rampages through the world—as, in a race,
The quadriga breaks through the starting gate,[22]
Plunging onto the course; the charioteer
Pulls vainly at the bit, is swept along—
The chariot can no longer feel the reins.

2.136–76

And yet, not even Media, whose groves
Cover the wealthy country, nor that land
Where lovely Ganges flows, nor Aeolis,
Whose river Hermus rushes dark with gold,
Can possibly compete with Italy
For praise—not Bactria, not India,
Not even all the incense-bearing sand
Of rich Panchaia. Here in Italy
It's true no bulls with nostrils snorting fire
Have plowed the soil; we've never sown the teeth
Of monstrous dragons, never harvested
A crop of men, bristling with countless spears
And helmets: here the land is filled with grain
And Bacchus' own liquid, Massic wine,
And olive oil, and healthy herds of cows.
Here the proud war-horse prances in the field;
From you, Clitumnus, come the snow-white flocks
And victim-bulls, bathed in your holy stream,
Who lead the Roman triumphs to the shrines
Of gods. Here is eternal spring, and here
Summer in winter's months; two times a year
The flocks are pregnant, and the apple trees
Bear fruit; no violent tigers wander here;
No savage lions breed; no aconite
Poisons unlucky pickers; no great snake
Darts with its scaly humps across the dirt
Or winds its giant folds into a coil.
Think of the mighty cities of this land,
Products of so much labor, and the towns
Piled up by hand on overhanging rocks,

22. Quadriga—a four-horse chariot.

With rivers flowing under their ancient walls.
Next, do I need to mention the two seas
Which wash our country, or her many lakes,
Great Como, or Lake Garda, you who heave
With swells and rumble like the sea? Should I
Describe the Lucrine Lake, her Julian gate,
Her sea dike locking out the angry waves
With their huge noise, where Caesar's water sounds
And echoes far-off surf, and where the swell
Of Tyrrhene waves is channeled into Lake
Avernus? Also, we have many streams
Of silver and of copper in our land
And veins of gold especially. And here
Grow vigorous tribes of men: Sabellians,
Marsians, Ligurians, who can withstand
Hardship, and Volscians with their little darts,
And heroes like the Decii, and great
Camillus, Marius, the Scipios,
And Caesar chief of all, who even now
Celebrates victory on Asian shores
And keeps the Eastern weaklings in their place
Far from the hills of Rome. Therefore, I sing:
Hail, Saturn's country, mighty mother of crops,
And mighty mother of men! It is for you
That I approach this subject, long the theme
Of praise and poetry; for you I dare
Unseal the long-closed holy well, and sing
Hesiod's song throughout the towns of Rome.

2.458–74

How lucky the farmers are—I wish they knew!
The Earth herself, most just, pours forth for them
An easy living from the soil, far off
From clashing weapons. Though the farmer has
No mansion with proud portals which spits out
A monster wave of morning visitors
From every room, nor do his callers gasp
At inlaid columns, bright with tortoiseshell,
Or gold-embroidered clothes or bronzes from
Ephyre, nor in his house is plain white wool
Dyed with Assyrian poison, nor does he
Corrupt his olive oil with foreign spice,
He has untroubled sleep and honest life.

Rich in all sorts of riches, with a vast
Estate, he has the leisure to enjoy
A cave, a natural pond, a valley where
The air is cool—the mooing of the cows
Is ever-present, and to sleep beneath
A tree is sweet. Wild animals abound
For hunting, and young people grow up strong,
Hardworking, satisfied with poverty;
Their gods are holy; parents are revered;
Surely, when Justice left the earth she stayed
Last with these folk, and left some tokens here.

HORACE

Q. Horatius Flaccus was born in 65 B.C. at Venusia, in southern Italy. His father was a freed slave, who wanted his son to have "as good an education as the child of any Roman senator or knight." He took the boy, therefore, to Rome, where he acted as his chaperone and moral guide, and he later sent him to Athens "to seek truth among the groves of Academe." While Horace was studying in Greece, Julius Caesar was assassinated. The twenty-year-old student joined the army of Brutus, and fought on the republican (losing) side at the battle of Philippi. Discouraged and impecunious, Horace returned to Rome, where he became a scribe in the Treasury. He began to write poetry (*Epodes* and *Satires*); he met Virgil and other young poets; finally, he was introduced to the rich, intellectual Maecenas, who became his patron and good friend, and who converted the young liberal into a faithful supporter and propagandist for the new empire. For the next thirty years, Horace lived the life of a genial, sophisticated success, a fat and gregarious bachelor, the friend of all the important people of his day. His first three books of *Odes* (in a wide variety of meters) were published in 23 B.C. Then he wrote his poetic *Epistles* (including the long "Art of Poetry") and a fourth book of *Odes*. He died in 8 B.C.

There always have been and are and will be those who don't like Horace, who feel that he lacks passion, or naturalness, or great original ideas. Some find his praises of Augustus offensive. Some are disappointed to find that there is affection and dislike in Horace, but little sex and violence. Some find him smug or pompous. Some find his Latin too difficult.

Indeed, he is the hardest Roman author to translate: His verse is very dense; it sometimes takes several lines of English to convey the sense, connotation, and imagery of one of his short phrases, and in this process of expansion the Horatian tone is lost. He does clever things with word order that are irreproducible in English. In *Odes* 1.5, for example, the first sentence says, literally, "What slim boy, dripping with liquid perfume, urges you, Pyrrha, among many roses, in a delightful cave?" The Latin language permits Horace, without losing the meaning, to mix up the boy, his perfume, the girl Pyrrha, the roses, and the cave totally, into a heady sexual emulsion, thus:

> What—many—slim—you—boy—among roses
> Dripping with liquid—urges—perfume
> In the delightful—Pyrrha—cave?

The sense of the boy's total involvement—seductive but stifling, passionate but "staged"—is reinforced by the word order. And Horace plays with two sets of images throughout the short poem. First is the set of "bright" versus "dark" words: Pyrrha means "fiery"; caves are dark; she has "yellow" hair; the boy will be amazed at the "black" storms; he believes her "golden"; she "shines" before she (like gold) is "tested" for purity. Second is the images of liquids: The boy "drips" with "liquid" perfume; Pyrrha, in Greek mythology, was the female survivor of the Great Flood; the boy will "weep"; he will be amazed at the rough "seas" of the affair; Horace, himself a former victim of Pyrrha's love, has hung up his "wet" clothes (perhaps dripping with perfume, like the boy's, in line one?) as an offering in the temple of the god of the "sea." Survivors of shipwrecks did this—but the storm Horace survived was, clearly, his affair with Pyrrha, and the unnamed sea-god is not Neptune, here, but Venus, who was, incidentally, born from the sea. There is also an untranslatable pun, which links the two sets of images: The boy believes Pyrrha is *aurea* ("golden"), but she is really a cheating *aura* ("wind"). It is a short, light poem on a fairly trivial subject (I wonder who's kissing her now? Poor guy!) But it is characteristic of Horatian craftsmanship at its best: the perfect words in the perfect order, arranged with formal elegance and a deliberately casual tone.

And so, opposed to the Horace-haters, there have always been Horace-lovers. They are a mixed group. Some like the *Satires* best, for their sensible moralizing, gentle humor, and Horace's lovable self-revelations. ("The Bore," by the way, is funnier and more pointed than most, if not all, of the rest.) Others prefer the public, patriotic Horace, for his noble tone and high political ideals. (Although I count myself a member of several of the "somes" and "others" of this paragraph, this particular group of "others" does not include me, and I am afraid I have rather neglected them in my choice of poems to include. I apologize.) Some like the thoughtful Horace, with his intelligent, practical Epicurean ethics. Others respond to the wit of Horace and his sophisticated observations about people and society. Some find his "classical" restraint and decorum appealing. And some worship his craft, his total power over words.

"I have set up a monument more undying than bronze, and higher than the pyramids," boasted Horace in *Odes* 3.30, "I shall not wholly die." His monument was the *Odes*, and he has not wholly died. Perhaps more than any other Roman, Horace was interested in posterity's opinion of him and his works. How pleased he would be to know that his poems have outlasted the empire with its pontifex and vestal virgins, that he is loved not only "beside the Rhone" but in lands he didn't know existed in the world, and that there are barbarian "knights and senators" who learn his language in order to read his polished verses and to learn what he thought about life!

SATIRE 1.9 ("THE BORE")

The other day I happened to be walking
Down Holy Street; my mind, as usual,[1]
Was totally absorbed in something or other.
Up runs this guy I scarcely know by name
And grabs my hand; "How *marvelous* to *see* you,"
He says; "Hey, how's it going?" "Not too bad,
Considering," I say; "Hope you're the same."
He's still beside me, so I add, "Can I
Do something for you?" But he says, "Come on,
You know me. I'm an intellectual."
"Well, good for you!" I say, and now (poor me)
I try to shake him, sometimes walking fast
Then stopping suddenly, and whispering
In my slave's ear, while perspiration drips
Down to my very feet. I say to myself
"I wish I had Bolanus' knack for rudeness!"

And all the while this nuisance rattles on
About each neighborhood, how *marvelous*
The city is. I never say a word,
And finally he says "You're terribly
Eager to be alone; I've noticed that
For quite a while. But never mind, I'm sticking
With you; I'll go as far as you are going."
"Oh no! It's out of your way. I'm going to
Visit a friend I don't believe you know.
He's sick, and lives a long way off, across
The Tiber, near the Gardens of Julius Caesar."
"That's quite all right! I've nothing else to do
And I'm not lazy; I'll come all the way."
My ears go down, just like a stubborn donkey's,
When he gets a load too heavy for his back.

He starts: "You know, if you *really* got to know me
You'd want me for your friend far more than Viscus
Or Varius. I mean, I can write more lines
Of poetry than anyone—and faster!
And dancing—how *attractively* I move
My—parts, and even Hermogenes would love
To sing like I do"—here, I interject,

1. Holy Street—the Sacred Way (*Via Sacra*), the main street in Rome.

"Do you have a mother, or other family,
Who need you at home?" "Not one," he says, "I've buried
All of them."

Lucky people! Now I'm left.
Finish me off; I see that doom impending
Which an old Sabine woman prophesied
To me as a child, when she shook the urn of fate:
NO POISON DIRE SHALL CARRY OFF THIS BOY
NOR SWORD OF ENEMY, NOR BELLYACHE,
NOR COUGH NOR LINGERING GOUT. HE'LL BE CONSUMED
BY A WILD BORE, ONE DAY. SO, FROM THE TIME
OF MANHOOD ON, LET HIM BEWARE OF TALKERS.[2]

Morning is almost over; we arrive
At the temple of Vesta; here, by chance, he has
A lawsuit pending, and he must respond
Today to the plaintiff, or default his case.
"Oh, please," he says, "Come with me, help me out
A little." I reply, "I'm damned if I have
The strength to stand! And I know nothing of
The law. I'm in a hurry; you know why."
"I wonder what to do," he says, "Should I
Abandon the case, or you?" "Oh please," I beg,
"Abandon me!" "I won't," says he, and starts
To walk ahead. It's hard to disobey
One's captor, so I follow.

He begins
Again, "How goes it with Maecenas and you?
Now there's a man with sense, and damn few friends.
And knows how to use his money! Hey, you'd have
A powerful ally, and an understudy,
If you'd just introduce him to yours truly;
In fact, I'll bet you'd clear the field of rivals."
"We don't behave the way you think, at his house.
No other clique's so free of jealousy;
If someone's richer, or knows more than I,
It doesn't damage me; each of us has
His special place." "Astonishing," he says,
"Hard to believe!" "But true." "You make me even
Hotter to join the group." "Well, give it a try.

2. Wild bore—I must admit that the bore-boar pun is not in the original
Latin. But how often does a translator get an opportunity like this?

You're so outstanding that you'll win, no doubt.
He's such a pushover, he has to make
It hard to get to him." "I'll never quit!
I'll bribe his slaves! If I'm refused today,
I won't give up. I'll find out the right time,
And meet him on the street, and follow him!
'Mortals win nothing big without great toil.'"

While he goes on like this, look who shows up!
Aristius Fuscus, my good friend, who knows
This fellow well. We stop. "How come you're here?
Where are you going?" All the usual.
I tug his cloak, I pinch his arm—it's quite
Insensitive—I nod, I roll my eyes
For him to save me. He's a comedian;
The stinker smiles, pretends he doesn't get it;
My insides boil with bilious rage. "But surely
You said you wanted a word with me *in private*?"
"Ah yes, I do remember, but I'll tell you
At a better time. Today's the thirtieth Sabbath:
We wouldn't want to offend the circumcised
Judaeans." "But," I say, "Religious scruples
Don't bother me a bit." "They bother *me*,"
He says, "I'm just a common man, and not
So strong as you. Forgive me; we will talk
Another time." Ay me, it's a black, black day!
The villain flees, and leaves me under the knife.

But then, by chance, the plaintiff in his lawsuit
Appears, and shouts, "You crook, where do you think
You're going?" then he turns to me and asks
"May I call you as a witness?" I consent
By giving my ear to touch. My "friend" is dragged [3]
Away to court, amid much bustling
And general noise. And so Apollo saved me!

3. By giving my ear to touch—an old legal custom.

ODES

1.5

What slender boy, his tunic soaked with scent,
On a mattress of roses, begs you to relent
In some romantic cavern, lady fair?
For whom do you tie up your yellow hair
So neatly, Pyrrha, artlessly demure?
Poor fool, who thinks your heart is so secure!

How many times he'll curse his luck, and cry,
And only half-believing, wonder why
The tranquil sea is rough and lashed with rain,
The gentle breeze is now a hurricane.
Naïvely, he believes you're solid gold,
And hopes you'll stay his darling, always cold
To propositions other fellows make;
He doesn't see his pitiful mistake.
Poor dazzled fools, who think, before they've tried you
That all the world is his, who sits beside you!

But from my vantage point, all safe and warm,
I thank the gods that I survived the storm;
There hang my wet clothes, for the deity
Of those who venture on that windswept sea.

1.9

Look there, how Mount Soracte stands, all white[4]
In deepest snow—the laboring forests will
No longer hold their burden up; the frost
Is piercing, and the rivers all stand still.

Let's melt the cold! Pile up a heap of logs
Upon the hearth, my Thaliarchus, and
From the Sabine bottle, pour us both a drink
Of unmixed four-year-old, with generous hand.

4. Mount Soracte—an isolated mountain (now Soratte) visible from the city
of Rome.

Leave all your other worries to the gods;
They can subdue the winds which, struggling, clash
With the wild sea—and stillness falls at once
Upon the cypress and the ancient ash.

Stop asking what tomorrow will be like;
Count as a dividend whatever Chance
Gives you of further days. You are a boy:
Do not neglect sweet loving, or the dance,

While your green youth is still untouched by grim
White hair; now let the vacant lot, the park
Attract the young again: the time is right
For them, and for soft whispers in the dark,

And now the lovely giggle of the girl
Betrays her secret hiding-place; the boy
Grabs at her ring or bracelet; she defends
Her prize, a while, then lets him have his toy.

I.11

It is not right, Leuconoë,
To know what things the gods decree,
What end for you, what end for me—
Please put your astral charts away,
And take our winters as they come,
And let Jove reckon up the sum.
This year, which sees the breakers drum
On broken cliffs before us, may
Be our last year. While we converse,
Age hurries on; put off her curse!
In life's clear dregless wine immerse
Your heart throw spun-out hopes away,
Don't trust Tomorrow; clutch TODAY.

I.22

The man of honor, free of guilty deeds
Requires no black man's darts or bow; he needs
No stock of toxic arrows to defend him,
Whether you send him

To Syrtis, with its sweating savage race,
Or Caucasus, a wild, unfriendly place,
Or Eastern regions, where (the legend goes)
Hydaspes flows.

I came upon a wolf, the other day,
As through the Sabine wood I made my way
Singing of Lalage, unarmed, unworried,
And off he scurried.
That wolf was huge, more rightly to be feared
Than any beast rough Daunia has reared,
Or any monster bred in Juba's home[5]
Where lions roam.

So put me on some barren northern plain
Where summer breezes never blow, where rain
And chilly fog and evil gusts may rend me,
Or you may send me
To lands where humans dare not live, for fear
Of Sol's bright car, which circles much too near:
In Lalage's sweet smile I will rejoice—
In her sweet voice.

1.23

Chloe, why do you run, just like a timid fawn,
Small, lone, lost in the hills, seeking the anxious doe?
Run, run, looking for mother!
Harsh winds scare it, and whistling trees.

One green lizard may creep over a snapping twig,
Loose leaves, bushes may swish, swept by a sudden blow,
Run, run, looking for mother,
Poor fawn, poor little wobbly knees!

I'm no tiger, my dear, seeking to crush his prey,
No fierce lion who hunts, stalking a trembling roe,
Grown girls don't run to mother,
Stop, now, wait for me, Chloe, please.

5. Juba's home—Africa.

1.37
"THE DEATH OF CLEOPATRA"

It is time now to tipple, to pound on the ground
With our feet all unfettered, and time for the priests
Those who frolic for Mars, to be hauling the gods
To their couches, my friends, for the ritual feasts.

Quite unthinkable up to this time to bring out
From our grandfathers' cellars the Caecuban wine
While the Queen was preparing sheer death for the empire
And crazy destruction for Jupiter's shrine,

Irrational, hoping for anything, everything
She, with her plague-riddled flock of half-men,
Was drunk on the sweetness of all her good luck,
But her ships plunged her down to sobriety, then

When scarcely a one came through safe from the fires
And her mind, full of terrified fantasies, fed
By the wine of her country, was dragged back to face
Real terror, by Caesar, who chased as she fled[6]

With his rowers from Italy—he like a hawk
And she, a soft dove, or a hare on the plains
Of the snowy north country, pursued at top speed
By a hunter—he wanted to put into chains

The fateful monstrosity. *She* wanted better,
To die like a hero, not frightened to face
A sword-point, not womanishly, she refused
To sail her fast ships off to some hiding-place;

She dared then to see with a tranquil expression
Her kingdom downfallen; she dared, too, to think
Of handling poisonous serpents, to take
To herself their black venom, her body's last drink.

In the mode of her dying most awesomely brave,
Deprived of her fierce fleet, it seems that she died
In this way, to avoid being dragged in a triumph
Proud woman! to gratify Caesar's own pride.

6. Caesar—here, Augustus, who defeated Cleopatra (and Antony) at the battle of Actium in 31 B.C.

1.38

Garlands, dear boy, woven on linden paper
Leave me cold; I hate Asiatic extras;
You must stop this searching for full-blown roses
Late in the autumn.

Please, take pains: work hard to refrain from adding
To the good, plain myrtle, which suits both you, who
Serve, and me, who lie in in the vine's dense shadow,
Drinking at leisure.

2.14

How speedily they pass, these years!
O Postumus, no pious praying
Wards off wrinkles, baldness, graying;
Death despises all your tears.

You think that daily sacrifice
Will keep a man from Pluto's hands [7]
Or from the Styx, which bounds his lands?
Three hundred bulls would not suffice.

No pious bribing can redeem
The humble worker of the earth,
Or save the man of royal birth,
We all must cross that mournful stream.

We flee the bloody clash of arms,
Avoid the smashing, roaring seas,
Shut out the wind which brings disease;
In vain, in vain we shun these harms.

For we must look, through dismal gloom,
On Danaeus' poor wretched daughters [8]
And Sisyphus, by hell's black waters,
Toiling up his hill of doom.

7. Pluto—god of the underworld; the Styx is an underworld river.
8. Danaeus's daughters—the legendary daughters of Danaeus, who murdered
their husbands, were punished by having to carry water in sieves. Sisyphus,
for some unknown (but heinous) offense, had to roll a stone up a hill; just as
he reached the top it always rolled down again.

You think that anxious care will save
Your trees in all their loveliness,
Your home, your wife? You will possess
Only the cypress on your grave.

A better owner will be found
For all your untouched, locked-up treasure,
He will drink in lavish measure;
Your rare old wine will drench the ground.

2.20

Transformed, through flowing air I'll travel then
When once these strange, strong wings begin to grow;
I'll fly above the land of jealous men,
And leave the towns below.

The Stygian wave will never hold me tight,
Not I, whose parents were so poor, not I
Your protégé, Maecenas, my delight:
I do not plan to die.

I soon will be in plumage, snowy pale,
My legs are getting horny, hard as leather,
And sprouting underneath this fingernail—
Look here! A downy feather.

More safe than Icarus, I'll wing along,[9]
A bird, to visit Africa's hot sands,
Or see the Bosporus—or take my song
To Hyperborean lands.

In Colchis and in Spain, in every place,
In Roman-hating Dacia, I'll be known;
Gelonians will know me, and the race
Who live beside the Rhone.

And for my empty funeral, I ask
For no disgraceful dirge, no air of gloom,
No sobs—and please omit the pointless task
Of building me a tomb.

9. Icarus—the son of Daedalus, who flew on homemade wings, too near the
sun; the wax that held his feathers together melted, and he fell into the sea.

3.26

In the battles of love I've fought well up to now
As for glory in war, I've my share—
Now it's time to retire the worn-out lover's lyre,
Put my arms on the wall, put them there.

Hang the torches up there, by the shapely left side
Of the Venus who sprang from the sea,
And the axes for breaking the doors of the ladies
Whose doors were not open to me.

Queen of Memphis and Cyprus, blest goddess, you hold
So much warmth, so much wealth, in your grip;
Grant me this: permit arrogant Chloe to feel
Just one little touch of your whip.

3.30

I have set up a monument, more undying
Than bronze, and higher then pyramids: no rage
Of storm can ruin it, nor rain, nor age
Of years uncountable, nor centuries flying.
I shall not wholly die; part of me will
Avoid the Goddess of Funerals. At least
I'll grow, refreshed by praise, so long as Priest
And silent Vestal climb the eternal hill.[10]
The land where Aufidus roars shall speak of me,[11]
Where Daunus, poor in water, was the king
Of farmers: I, once poor, had power to sing
The first Aeolian songs in Italy[12]
Muse, you have earned the praise: be prideful now
And bind Apollo's laurels on my brow.

10. Priest and silent Vestal—the highest priest of the Roman state religion
was called the Pontifex Maximus (which means, literally, "biggest bridge-
maker"); the Vestal Virgins were the priestesses of Vesta, the goddess of the
hearth. "The eternal hill" is the Capitoline, on which stood the temple of
Jupiter.
11. Aufidus—a river (now the Ofanto) in Apulia, where Horace was born.
Daunus was the legendary king of the land.
12. Aeolian songs—Greek lyric meters.

4.1

After so many years, will you start again
That warfare? Spare me, Venus, spare the pain.
I once lived under good Queen Cinara's
Kind rule, but I am not the man I was.
Harsh mother of sweet love, stop trying, now,
To bend my fifty years, too stiff to bow
To your mild orders. Go, where young men pray
More charmingly—a better place to stay
Is Paulus Maximus' house, if your desire
Is for a suitable heart to set on fire.
Drive, with your purple swans, to him, for he
Is handsome and well born, and vigorously
Defends his anxious clients. Skillful in
A hundred arts, he'll carry your flag and win
Your battles everywhere. You'll help him beat
Rich rivals, and he'll smile at their defeat
And set up marble trophies, for your sake,
Roofed with sweet citrus wood, by the Alban Lake.
There'll be incense to sniff, and songs to suit
Your taste: the lyre and Berecynthian flute[13]
And panpipes will delight you; there, twice daily
The boys and tender girls will hymn you, gaily
Dancing to praise the holy power of passion
And leaping with bare white feet, in Salian fashion.[14]

I can no longer care for things like these.
No trusting faith in mutual love can please
Me now, no boy nor woman. To spend the hours
In drinking contests, or to weave fresh flowers
To crown my temples bores me now. But why,
Why, Ligurinus, tell me, why do I
Who never weep, feel tears upon my cheek?
Why, when my facile tongue begins to speak
Does it fail me suddenly, and bring me shame?
In my nightly dreams I have you, caught and tame,
Then you fly off again; I follow you
Wherever you are going; I pursue
Your cruel flight, pleading, in constant motion,
Over the grassy fields, over the ocean.

13. Berecynthian flute—a curved flute used in the worship of the Phrygian
mother-goddess Cybele.
14. Salian—the Salii were priests of Mars, who did leaping dances in their
worship.

4·7

Routed, the snows retreat; now, grass
Retakes the fields, and on bald trees
New leaves are growing.
The earth is changed; the swollen streams
Subsiding, and between their banks,
Calmly are flowing.
The grateful sister Graces dare
To go out naked, and with Nymphs
To dance and play.
"*You* may not hope to be reborn,"
The year warns, and the hours that snatch
Each kindly day.
West winds soften the cold, then Spring
Is ousted by the Summer, who
Herself grows old,
And yields to fruitful Fall, who pours
Grain in our laps, then soon gives way
To deadening cold.
Celestial wounds are quickly healed,
The moons make whole their damaged parts,
But we, who must
Go down where father Aeneas, Ancus,
And wealthy Tullus are, become[15]
Shadows and dust.
Who knows if the high gods will add
More time tomorrow, to today's
Numerable whole?
The only gifts which flee the hands
Of greedy heirs are those you give
To your dear soul.
Torquatus, once you die and hear
Your case summed up (most brilliantly)
By Minos, then[16]
Your wit, your goodness, your high birth
Will not restore you, exiled from
The world of men.
Diana could not free her pure
Hippolytus from shadowy hell,[17]
He died in the end.

15. Aeneas—mythical ancestor of the Romans; Tullus, Ancus—legendary
third and fourth kings of Rome.
16. Minos—king of Crete. He became one of the judges in the underworld.
17. Hippolytus—the son of Theseus. A chaste youth, devoted to the goddess

Theseus was strong, but could not break [18]
The chains of oblivion that held
His best-loved friend.

4·9

I have a jar of Alban wine, which has
Outlived nine years; in my garden, you will find
Parsley for weaving, Phyllis, and an army
Of ivy; when you bind

Your hair with this, you'll sparkle. My whole house
Is smiling with silver plate; the altar, all
Tied up with holy boughs, is hungry for
The slaughtered lamb to fall.

All hands are hurrying; now here, now there,
Servants are running, boys mixed up with girls,
The flames are quivering and sending up
The sooty smoke in curls.

What festival is this, which you're invited
To celebrate with me? This day divides
The month of the goddess born at sea, the month
Of Venus, April's Ides: [19]

Just as significant for me as my
Own birthday, rightfully this time appears
Almost more sacred: from this dawn Maecenas
Numbers his flowing years.

Telephus, whom you want, is occupied
By one from a higher class than yours, a teasing
Amorous heiress, and she holds him captive
In bonds that he finds pleasing.

Diana (Greek Artemis); his stepmother Phaedra loved him; he rejected her.
She committed suicide and left a message accusing Hippolytus of rape, where-
upon Theseus hastily cursed his son, and Hippolytus was dragged to death by
his own horses.

18. Theseus—the hero who killed the Minotaur. One of his more foolish
exploits was his attempt, with his dear friend Pirithoos, to kidnap Per-
sephone, the queen of the underworld. Theseus managed to escape, but Pi-
rithoos remained in hell.

19. Ides—the fifteenth of the month.

The fall of burned-up Phaeton should discourage [20]
Ambitious hopes, and winged Pegasus [21]
Weighed down by his earthborn rider, should provide
A heavy warning to us.

Always seek your own level; it is not
Permitted us to hope for things above
What's suitable for us. Now, Phyllis, come
To me, my final love—

From now on, I will never burn again
For any other woman—sing along
With me, in your loved voice, for sorrow's darkness
Is lightened by a song.

20. Phaeton—drove the chariot of the sun-god (his father) and crashed.
21. Pegasus—the winged horse, ridden by Bellerophon.

PROPERTIUS

Sextus Propertius was born in about 50 B.C., probably at Asisium (the modern Assisi). He moved to Rome as a young man, studied law for a short time, fell in love, wrote a popular book of love elegies, and became one of the protégés of Maecenas (the patron also of Horace and Virgil). He wrote at least three more volumes of poetry; the fourth, which is concerned less with love (and more with Roman history and religion) than the first three, was written in 16 B.C. or later. Propertius may have married and been a father. We do not know when he died.

The great love of his life was "Cynthia." Her real name was Hostia; her social and marital status are not clear: All we can say for certain, because Propertius tells us so, is that she was "not chaste." However, although we know less about Cynthia's biography than we do about that of Catullus's Lesbia, we know far more about her as a person. She is, in fact, one of the first (one of the only?) subjects of love poems to be described as a distinctive human being, not merely as an object on which the poet hangs his passion and his songs. Cynthia was tall, with bright dark eyes and blonde (artificially colored) hair; she was well educated and musical, she liked poetry and perhaps wrote some. She was also passionate, hot-tempered, and bossy. Both she and Propertius were constantly unfaithful to each other, but each expected and demanded fidelity from the other. The result was that they fought a lot; scratching, hitting, and wrestling were, it seems, a standard—and for these lovers a delightful—feature of their relationship. Apparently they were always breaking up and being reunited, but through it all, Cynthia remained the dominant force in Propertius's poetry.

Even in the fourth book, the two best poems are the only two about Cynthia, although, apparently, she had died before they were written. However, an intriguing theory about her death in 4.7, first proposed (*Classical Review*, May 1937) by Agnes Lake (Michels) and suggested to me by James Zetzel, is that Cynthia was not dead when this grisly, moving poem was written. It is quite possible: A striking feature of Propertius's poetry is his obsession with fantasies about deaths, funerals, burials, and tombstones, both his own and Cynthia's.

Love and poetry writing are often identified and used as symbols for each other in Roman verse, particularly in Horace and Virgil. They are so, too, in Propertius, for example in 1.18, which is so full of allusions to writing and song that it almost seems not to be about love at all. But Propertius is not a sterile navel-contemplator, writing about writing. Although sometimes his references to mythology seem a bit excessive to the modern reader, he is an exquisite craftsman, and his craft—with its consummate combination of specific detail, subtle imagery, humor, melancholy, thoughtful abstraction, and rhetorical power—allows him to make the strongest, most moving statements possible about his divinely impossible love.

ELEGIES

1.3

Exhausted as the girl of Cnossus, lying[1]
Prone on the empty shore
While Theseus sailed away;
Or like Andromeda, when she lay down[2]
For her first sleep, at last
Freed from the flinty rocks;
Tired as a Thracian Bacchant, who has danced
Until she drops, beside
The grassy riverbed;
So Cynthia seemed to breathe soft peace, asleep
Reclining, on her couch,
Her head propped on her hands.

I dragged my drunken footsteps there so late
The slave boy had to shake
His torch to keep a light.
I tried to tiptoe softly to her couch
(Though drunk, I hadn't yet
Entirely lost my head),
Desire and Wine, two potent deities,
Began to make me hot
And ordered me to take
Her gently in my arms, and move her hand
And kiss her, then move in
And try to take the fort;
But I was scared to break my mistress' peace
And didn't try; I know
How savage she can be.
I stood there, glued, and fixed my eyes on her
Like Argus, staring at
Io's peculiar horns.[3]

1. Girl of Cnossus—Ariadne, daughter of King Minos of Crete. She helped
the hero Theseus to escape from the labyrinth, and was later deserted by him.
2. Andromeda—was saved from a monster by the hero Perseus, who later
deserted her.
3. Argus—a hundred-eyed herdsman set to guard Io, a maiden loved by Zeus
(Lat. Jupiter). She had been turned into a heifer.

Once, Cynthia, I took the leafy crown
From my own brow and placed
The garland on your head,
And then I played at forming curls, with your
Loose hair, then gave to you
Some pilfered apples, gifts
Which, lavished on Ungrateful Sleep, rolled down
Out of your sloping lap
Over and over again.
When, once in a while, you sighed or moved, I was
Appalled, and foolishly
Believed it was a sign
That you were seeing strange and frightening dreams,
That someone in your dream
Was taking you by force.

The moon passed by your open window then,
Officiously at work
Flashing her lingering lights,
With those thin rays she opened your shut lids
And Cynthia, leaning on
Her elbow, spoke to me:

"So, *finally*, you've come back to my bed,
Forced by some other girl
Who locked the door on you!
Where did you waste this night that was to be
For me, while all the stars
Rolled by, and wore you out?
You beast, I wish you'd have to suffer through
The kind of lonely night
You always make me spend!

"I worked some time at the loom to keep awake
Then, bored with that, I took
My lyre, and sang a while
Complaining softly to myself, that you
Desert me and spend hours
Loving another girl.
Then happy Sleep flew down and mastered me
And put an end to tears
And stopped my painful thoughts."

1.8b

She's here! She swears she'll stay! You jealous fools,
Rupture your guts! I've won!
My prayers have worn her down.
You lusting Malice, stifle your empty joy;
My Cynthia will not
Be sailing anywhere.
I am her love, and Rome is lovable
For my sake. Without me,
She says, no kingdom could
Be sweet to her, for she would rather share
My narrow bed, and be
Mine, in whatever way,
Than win the realm of Hippodamia[4]
And all the ancient wealth
The Elean horses won.

Although he offers much, may offer more,
She'll never, greedily,
Leave my embrace for his.
I won her not with gold, nor Indian pearls,
I served her humbly, with
Entrancing poetry.

The Muses and Apollo do exist!
I lean on them; unique
Cynthia is my own!
Now I could walk among the highest stars:
Whether the daylight comes
Or night, she is my own!
No rival now can shake my solid love,
This glory will remain
And know my white-haired Age.

1.18

Here is a silent and deserted place
Where I may grieve aloud.
Only the soft West Wind
Visits this empty grove: I can publish, here,

4. Hippodamia—daughter of the king of Elis. Pelops won her hand in a
chariot race.

My hidden sorrows, if
These solitary rocks
Are able to keep secrets. Cynthia,
Tell me, when did you start
Rejecting me? And when
Did I first make you cry, my Cynthia?
Not long ago, I was
Among the happy in love,
But now your letter of censure casts me out.
Do I deserve this? Whose
Witchcraft or songs have changed
Your love for me? Or was it some new girl
You thought I loved? *You* are
The fickle one: I swear
By the love I hope to win again from you
No other dainty feet
Have danced into my house.
The pain you've caused should make me bitter; yet
I'd never let my rage
Become so cruel that
I'd give you cause for anger against me
Or make your brilliant eyes
Ugly with streaming tears.

Or is it that the tropes of love (the blush,
The pallid cheek) do not
Appear upon my face
And cry out to the world that I am yours?
Here are my witnesses:
(If trees know love at all)
This beech tree and this pine, the mistress of
Arcadia's poet-god;
How many times my words
Have echoed in the softness of your shade,
How often "Cynthia"
Is carved into your bark!

How many times you've injured me, my love,
Only your silent door
Can tell; I have been meek
Enduring your most insolent commands,
Never indulging in
An eloquent complaint.
And my reward? This spring, this chilly rock,

Enforced retirement, in
This uncouth wilderness;
Whatever I could tell, out of my grief,
I'm forced to sing, alone,
To the free-singing birds.
But even here, let "Cynthia" resound
And fill the empty rocks
Forever with your name.

2.7

The marriage law's annulled; my Cynthia
Is overjoyed! When first
That law was published, we
Both wept for hours, fearing that we might
Be separated, though
Not even Jupiter
Can part, against their wishes, two who love.
"But Caesar's powerful,"
You said. But Caesar is
Powerful chiefly on the battlefield;
To conquer nations brings
No special power in love.

I'd sooner have my head hacked from my neck
Than trade our fire for
A wedding torch, and glance
Back at your door as I go past, a groom
With tear-dimmed eyes, your door
Tight shut, betrayed by me.
The sound of wedding flutes would bring you dreams
Grimmer than those induced
By trumpets at the grave.

How could I furnish sons for the triumphs of
The fatherland? I swear
No soldier ever will
Come from my blood. I'll follow the true camp
Of Cynthia; and then
Not even Castor's horse
Will match my stature; here, in the field of love
My name, my glory lies,
Fame that has traveled far

As the wintry Borysthenidae. My love,
You are the only one
Who pleases me; may I
Alone please you, my Cynthia. This love
Will always be, for me,
Greater than fatherhood.

2.11

Others may write about you, if they want,
Or leave you out, ignored;
That man should praise you who
Wishes to sow his seed in sterile soil.
Believe me, all your gifts
Will burn up, on your bier
On that black final day, along with you.
The traveler will walk
Over your grave, and not
Notice your bones, nor will he stop and say
"One time these ashes were
An educated girl."

2.15

O my good luck! O night, shining for me!
And o you little bed,
Blessed by my happiness!
How long we talked and talked while the lamp was lit;
And when the light was gone
What a splendid fight we had;
For now she wrestled, with her nipples bare,
Then pulled her tunic on
Covered up, stopped me short.
My eyes were heavy with sleep; she opened them
With her lips, and said to me
"Up with you, lazybones!"
How many shifting poses we assumed,
How long my kisses lay
Delaying, on your lips.

The joys of Venus should not go to waste
In sightless fumbling; eyes
Are the generals in love's war.
Paris, they say, succumbed to the Spartan wife[5]
Chancing to see her nude
Fresh from her husband's bed.
And Phoebus' sister's said to have been won[6]
By nude Endymion;
Naked, she slept with him.
If you, hardhearted, go to bed in clothes,
Through your ripped nightgown you
Will feel my hands. In fact,
If you provoke me further, if you tease
Too much, you'll have to show
Your mother your bruised arms.
Your breasts, young and erect, should not prevent
Your play; you've borne no child
No shame is in those breasts.

While Fate allows, let's glut our eyes with love;
The Long Night's coming; Day
Will not return for us.
I wish you'd bind us here, embracing, one,
With chains that are too strong
For any day to break.
Let doves be your example; they are bound
The female and the male
United in one love.
It's wrong to look for a boundary to love's
Insanity; true love
Doesn't know limits or ends.
Earth will mock the farmer with winter fruit
Sooner, and Sol will drive[7]
The horses of the Night,
Rivers call back their waters to the source
And the fish die of thirst
In the dry sea, before
I'll transfer to another my love and pain;
Hers I shall be alive,
In death, I shall be hers.

5. Spartan wife—Helen of Troy.
6. Phoebus's sister—Diana (Greek Artemis). She fell in love with Endymion, a beautiful boy who had been condemned to perpetual sleep.
7. Sol—the sun-god.

But if she gives me other nights like this
With her, a year will be
Long enough life for me.
If she gives many such, I'll never die;
Even one night like this
Can make a man a god.

If all men wanted such a life as ours
And lay, with limbs weighed down
By the pure wine of love,
There'd be no cruel steel, no ships of war,
Our bones would not be tossed
In the sea at Actium;[8]
And Rome, so often plagued with triumph-cries
Over her own, could cease
To tear her hair and mourn.
Posterity can give my sort this praise;
Our wine-cups never did
Injury to the gods.

While it is light, do not desert the fruit
Of life; if you give all
Your kisses, still, they're few.
See, leaves are dropping from the withered crowns;
They swim there, in the cups
All strewn about; so, we
Who now are lovers, full of hope, may find
Tomorrow's dawn, for us,
Will close the door on life.

4·7

So: maybe there are ghosts, and Death does not
End all; a glowing shadow
Flies from the conquered pyre.
For Cynthia appeared and lay upon
My couch—she, lately buried
Beside the humming highway,
While Sleep was hovering, and hanging on
My passion's funeral,

8. Actium—the climactic battle (31 B.C.) in which Augustus defeated Antony and Cleopatra.

And I, complaining that
My bed—my former kingdom—was now cold.
Her hair, on which she prided
Herself, was still the same;
So were her eyes, but the dress upon her body
Was burnt, and fire had nibbled
Her favorite beryl ring;
Lethe's water had worn away her lips.[9]
She still had breath and voice
But on her fragile hands
The thumb-bones rattled accusingly at me:

"Traitor!—but girls can hope
For nothing better from men—
Does sleep have power over you so soon?
Have you forgotten already
The stolen times we had
In the Subura, where the night is not[10]
For sleeping? Or my window
Worn by our nightly frauds,
Through which, for you, so many times I hung
On a rope, and hand over hand
Climbed down into your arms?
We often worshipped Venus at some crossroad;
Our clothing made the highway
Under our mingled breasts
Grow hot. I mourn for the wordless treaty, whose
False words were snatched away
Destroyed by the deaf South Wind!

"Yet no one cried out for my eyes, as I
Was going; if you'd called,
You might have given me
Another day with you; no watchman shook
His cane to guard my body,
My head, exposed, was wounded
By a broken tile. Who saw you bent with grief
At my funeral? Who saw you

9. Lethe—river in the underworld; the shades of the dead drank its water and
forgot their past lives. Its amnesiac properties apparently didn't work on
Cynthia.
10. The Subura—a part of Rome, frequented by prostitutes and other low
types in the city.

Wear black, and warm your toga
With tears? If going farther than the door
Embarrassed you, at least
You might have ordered that
My bier be carried slowly. Faithless man,
You should have prayed for winds
To fan my pyre. And why
Were the flames not sweet with incense? But if this
Was too expensive, still,
You might have scattered some
Wild hyacinths upon me, and appeased
My ashes with some wine
From a cracked jar—quite cheaply

"Burn Lygdamus! Let branding irons glow
For the homeborn slave. I knew
When I drank the treacherous wine
That turned me pale. And clever Nomas—let her
Conceal her magic potions;
The broken jug, still fiery,
Shows she is guilty, too. And as for *her*,
Who once was open to
The public, for inspection
And sold her nights so cheaply—now the heavy
Gold border of her dress
Inscribes upon the ground
Her great importance! If a gossipy slave
Mentions my beauty, she
Repays the girl unfairly
With heavier wool to spin; old Petale,
Who took wreaths to my grave
Is chained to a filthy tree stump;
And Lalage is hung by her twisted hair
And beaten, since she dared
To use my name, when asking
A favor. You allowed that whore to melt
My image of gold, and get
A dowry from my pyre
As it burned. But still, Propertius, I will not
Reproach you, though you do
Deserve it, for I know
I reigned a long time in your poetry.

"I swear now, by the song
That cannot be rewritten,
The song of the Fates, that I kept faith with you
And may the dog of Hell
Howl softly if my words
Are true; but if I lie, then may a serpent
Hiss at my sepulcher
And sleep upon my bones.

"Hell's sordid river leads to two allotted
Regions, and every soul
Rows one way or the other:
One boat is carrying Clytemestra's crime; [11]
Another holds the wooden
Monstrosity of Crete,[12]
The unreal cow—but look! some of the crowd
Are swept away in a wreathed
Skiff, to a place where blessed
Breezes ruffle the roses of Elysium,[13]
Where many lyres, and round
Cymbals of Cybelle
And Lydian harps are making music for
The turbaned dancers. There,
Two faithful wives, great souls,
Andromeda and Hypermestra, tell [14]
Their stories: the first complains
That chains—her mother's fault—
Have bruised her arms, and her pure hands were tied
To icy rocks; the second
Tells of her sisters' daring
And that she was too weak for such a crime.
Thus, with death's tears we cure
Life's loves; but I conceal
The many crimes of your unfaithfulness.

11. Clytemestra—usually spelled Clytemnestra. She murdered her husband
Agamemnon on his return from the Trojan War.
12. Monstrosity of Crete—Pasiphaë, wife of King Minos, fell in love with a
bull and hid inside a fake cow (the monstrosity) to attract him. By this bull,
she became the mother of the Minotaur, which lived in the labyrinth.
13. Elysium—legendary land of the blessed. But the more usual Greek and
Roman view was that almost everyone, good or bad, went to the regular,
depressing underworld after death.
14. Andromeda, Hypermestra—for Andromeda, see fn. 2 above. Hyper-
mestra was the only daughter of Danaeus who did not murder her husband.
See "Horace," fn. 8.

"Now hear, if I have moved you,
If Chloris' magic herbs
Don't own you totally: give to my nurse
Parthenie, in her
Shaky old age, whatever
She needs—she served you gladly, without thought
Of profit. And my dear
Latris, whose very name
Means 'service': do not let her hold the mirror
For a new mistress. Then,
Whatever verses you
Have written about me, let them be burned
For me; stop getting praise
Which rightfully is mine.

"Now, from my tomb expel the hostile clumps
Of ivy, which with twisting
Leaves bind my soft bones.
And there, where the fruitful Anio makes his bed [15]
Among the orchards, where
By the will of Hercules
Ivory never yellows, set up a pillar
And write on it these verses
Worthy of me, but brief,
So that the city people who ride by
Can read them without stopping
Their hurrying chariots:
HERE GOLDEN CYNTHIA LIES, IN TIBUR'S EARTH:
NOW, ANIO, NEW PRAISE
IS ADDED TO YOUR BANKS.

"Do not reject a dream that comes through holy
Gates; if a dream has goodness
It also carries weight.
Nightly we wander everywhere; the night
Sets free the captive shades
And even Cerberus
Unlocked, runs loose. At dawn the law returns us
To Lethe's pools; the boatman
Checks his passenger list.

15. Anio—a tributary stream of the Tiber (now called *Teverone*), noted for
the beauty of its surrounding countryside, particularly at Tibur.

"Let other women have you now; soon I
Alone will hold you; you
Will be with me, and we
Will mingle bone with bone, and wear them thin."

When she had finally
Finished attacking me,
The spirit disappeared from my embrace.

TIBULLUS

Three volumes of elegiac poetry have come down to us under the name of Tibullus. In the first volume the lady chiefly celebrated is named Delia; Nemesis is the mistress of the second volume, but Tibullus's poetic love life (with boys as well as girls) is quite complicated. The third volume contains more love elegies, but most or all of them are probably not by Tibullus.

The poet, whose name was apparently Albius Tibullus, lived from about 54 to 19 B.C., and was a member of a Roman literary circle patronized by the general and statesman Messalla Corvinus.

Tibullus has the distinction of being the only minor poet in this volume. There are those, of course, who would be angry with this statement. Some of them are devoting their professional lives to studying Tibullus; in fact, the reader may be pleased (or amused) to learn that classical scholars are at this very moment in the midst of a Tibullus revival, as a result of which new beauties of thought, of expression, and particularly of structure are being discovered almost daily. There *is* grace and polish and symmetry in Tibullus's works, certainly, for which he was much admired in his own day. The poem translated here (the first of his elegies) is also noteworthy in that it could serve as a good introduction to classical Latin poetry. Indeed, it is almost a *summary* of other Roman poetry; this elegy treats nearly every theme that appears frequently in the major poets: the folly of greed, ambition, war, and seafaring; the superiority of the country life (simple, pious, and old-fashioned) over urban moneygrubbing and extravagance; the contrast of present day with past, and poet with his ancestors; the importance of good sound sleep and plenty of food; the bittersweet "slavery" and "warfare" that love brings; the fascination with death and funerals; the pressing need to gather rose-buds in one's youth and the unseemliness of white-haired lovers; the obsession with two goals that the poet consciously rejects but cannot seem to stop talking about, money and reputation. Perhaps the only major Roman theme not touched on here is the power of poetry.

Otherwise, it's all here, classical Latin poetry in a nutshell, smoothly, elegantly expressed. And almost nothing more: nothing difficult, or quirky, or wild, or funny, or indecorous, or different. And that is why I call Tibullus a minor poet.

ELEGY 1.1

Let others pile up wealth, in yellow gold
Or in vast acreage
Of excellent topsoil,
Let constant struggling with hostile neighbors
Scare others, and the loud
War trumpets spoil their sleep;
But let my poverty bring me a life
Of laziness, so long as
My hearth stays bright with fire.

When the time is right I'll plant the tender vines
And the broad fruit trees, at
A peasant's dawdling pace,
And may Hope stay with me, and bring me heaps
Of fruit, and storage vats
Brimming with strong new wine.
For I am reverent; I crown with flowers
Tree stumps, forsaken in
The fields, and ancient stones
Which stand at crossroads; every year I give
The first fruits of my crop
To the farmer's deity.

Yellow-haired Ceres, may my farm produce[1]
A spiky crown, to hang
Before your temple doors;
May red Priapus, watchman of the orchard,[2]
Scare all the birds away
With his vicious pruning hook.
And you too, Lares, once the guardians[3]
Of prosperous acres, now
Poor ones, bring me your gifts.
A heifer, then, was sacrificed for the welfare
Of countless steers; these days,
A little lamb is killed
For the thin soil. A lamb shall fall for you;

1. Ceres—Greek Demeter, goddess of grain and fertility.
2. Priapus—a fertility god. Statues of him, with enormous phalluses, stood watch over orchards and gardens.
3. Lares—Roman gods of the household, with no Greek counterpart. They may originally have been ghosts of the family's ancestors, or fertility deities.

And country boys around it
Will shout "Ho! Lares; bring us
Big harvests and good wine!"

                                   But as for me,
May I be content to live
On little, and avoid
The need for distant journeys. I'll escape
The heat of the Dogstar's rising
Beside a flowing stream
In a tree's shadow; I won't be too proud
To hold a hoe, sometimes,
Or stir up lazy cows
With a prod, nor be embarrassed to bring home
In my arms a lamb or kid
Forgotten by its mother.
Please spare my little flock, you thieves and wolves;
Gather your booty from
A greater herd than mine;
From these must come the yearly offering
To purify my shepherd;
From these must come the milk
To sprinkle for mild Pales. Stay with me,
You gods, do not reject
Gifts from a humble table
Or from clean earthenware: in ancient times
Farmers first made such cups
Molded from simple clay.

I do not ask for the riches of my fathers
Or the profits that they reaped
From harvests, long ago;
A small crop is enough; it is enough
If I may lie in bed
And give myself a rest
On the familiar couch. How good to hear
The cruel winds, while I
Am lying there, and holding
My mistress in my loving arms! How pleasant
When winter winds are pouring
Cold showers down, to sleep
Securely, aided by the sound of rain!
This is my choice; let others
Get rich, deservedly,
If they can bear harsh storms and raging seas.

I'd sooner see the world's
Supply of gold destroyed
And every emerald, than have one girl
Crying because of my
Departure on some trip.

For you, Messalla, it's appropriate
To fight, on land and sea,
And to display at home
Your captured trophies. I've been captured, too:
Held fast and chained up by
The beauty of a girl.
I sit, a doorman, at her cruel doors.
My Delia, fame is nothing
To me: as long as I
Can be with you, I'm happy to be called
Lazy and unambitious.

Just let me look at you
When my last hour has come, and as I die,
Let me hold on to you
As my arms lose their strength.
My Delia, you will cry to see me placed
On the bed that is to burn;
You'll give me kisses mixed
With tears. You'll cry: your breast is not bound up
By links of steel; no flint
Is in that tender heart.
And from that funeral no soft young girl
Or young man will be able
To come away dry-eyed.
But, Delia, have some pity for my ghost:
Spare your loose-flowing hair;
Don't scratch those tender cheeks.

Meanwhile, as long as fate allows, let's join
In love; for too soon Death
Dark-veiled, will come to us,
And idle Age come creeping; it will be
Unseemly to make love
Or speak seductive words
When our hair is white. But now's the time to deal
With easy Venus, while
We can, without a blush,
Break down a door or start a lovers' quarrel;

Here, I'm a general,
Here a good fighting man.

You, flags and trumpets, get away from here;
Bring wounds to greedy men,
And bring them riches. I,
Safe with my gathered harvest, shall look down
On hunger, and, secure,
I shall look down on wealth.

OVID

Publius Ovidius Naso was born in 43 B.C. His family was of eques-
trian ("knight's") rank; he was a native of Sulmo, about ninety miles
from Rome. He was educated in Rome and Athens. Like most well-
off young men of his day, he studied rhetoric, in order to prepare for a
legal and perhaps political career, but his talent for easy, mellifluous
versification became apparent very early: "Whatever I wrote," he tells
us, "turned into poetry." He fit right in with the literary crowd in
Rome, and his love elegies made him instantly popular. He wrote
easily, and over the next thirty years or so produced several volumes
of love poetry ("The Loves"), a volume of fictitious "Love-letters of
Famous Women," a work on cosmetics, a titillating work on seduc-
tion and lovemaking called "The Art of Love," its sequel "The Cures
for Love," the unfinished "Calendar of Festivals," "Medea" (a trag-
edy, now lost), and the fifteen-volume *Metamorphoses*. He was mar-
ried three times; apparently the third marriage was a good one.

In A.D. 8 this lively, happy, urban sophisticate was exiled from
Rome forever. The emperor Augustus ordered him to be "relocated"
to Tomi, a bookless, unhealthy, dangerous outpost on the Black Sea.
It is unclear what Ovid's crime was: He tells us that he was banished
because of a book and because of something he "saw." The book,
clearly, was the erotic, amoral "Art of Love," which was not re-
garded, somehow, as quite fitting in with the spirit of the emperor's
new crusade for the reform of Roman sexual ethics. What he "saw" is
still unknown. Ovid was wretched in Tomi, but he kept working. He
learned two of the barbarian languages spoken in the district; in fact,
he complained that he was forgetting his Latin. He wrote five books
of verse lamentations, called "The Sorrows," four books of "Letters
from the Black Sea," a work on fish and other wild life of the region,
and a poem—in praise of Augustus!—in the Getic language. He kept
hoping for a pardon. But it never came; in A.D. 18, he died.

As a poet, Ovid has some obvious faults. He is easy to read (a
virtue), but he is less rewarding to reread. He is wordy; he never uses
three words when ten will do. He is rhetorical; his balanced con-

trasts, neat wordplays, and legalistic arguments are carried too far and make his work sound artificial. Sometimes his cleverness turns into cuteness. The "Corinna" of his elegies does not seem like a real person. His versification is so easy and smooth that it can get boring.

But for all that, Ovid's charm is also obvious. The *Metamorphoses*, a collection of myths from the Creation to the astrification of Julius Caesar, is a wonderful book. The poet is a fine storyteller, and the stories he tells are in themselves fine. His verse is rapid, easy on the ear, lush and lovely; his eye for convincing and dramatic detail is sharp; his amused, detached, tongue-in-cheek irreverence has appealed to innumerable readers. In fact, Ovid has always been a popular poet; of the Romans, his influence is probably second only to Virgil's. Victorian critics disapproved of him for his "insincerity"; his crime, in their eyes, was that his Attitude Was Not Serious. Serious readers, therefore, are advised to skip Ovid; all others are encouraged to enjoy him.

AMORES ("THE LOVES")

1.4

Your husband's going to the dinner, too?
I'd love it if that meal
Could prove to be his last!
So, I can only *look* at my sweet girl
Like any other guest,
While he has all the fun
Of being touched, and getting warm when you
Recline close to his chest?
And, when he wants, he'll fling
An arm around your neck? I'm not surprised
That Hippodamia's charm[1]
Stirred up the semi-men
To battle, after wine. My home is not
The woods; my limbs are not
Stuck on a horse's body;
But I can scarcely keep my hands off you!
Now here's what you must do,
And don't let the East Wind
Or tepid South Wind carry off my words:
Arrive before him. Why?
No reason. Still, come first.
When he reclines, you'll join him on the couch,
Your face all innocence,
But secretly, you'll touch
My foot with yours. Then, watch my nods—my face
Will speak to you; observe
My furtive signals, then
Return them. I shall speak loquaciously
Without a voice; my brows
Will speak, and you may read
Words from my fingers, words marked down in wine.
If you are thinking of
Some sexy fun we've had
Touch your soft thumb against your blushing cheek.
But if it happens that
You're irrigated with
Some little thing that I have done or said,

1. Hippodamia—her wedding was the occasion for a drunken battle between
the (human) Lapiths and the (half-equine) Centaurs.

But cannot say it, tug
Gently upon your ear.
But if I do or say some things you like—
Light of my life!—then slide
Your ring around and around.
If you touch the table as one does in prayer
You're praying for That Man
To get what he deserves.
Be smart; tell *him* to drink the wine he's mixed
And murmur to a slave
To pour you what you want.
I'll snatch the cup you hand him, and be first
To drink from the same place
Where you have drunk before.
If He by chance should pass you something which
He's tasted first, reject
The food that's touched his mouth.
Don't let him lay his arm around your neck,
And don't rest your sweet head
Against his bony chest.
Don't let your clothing or those yielding nipples
Admit his fingers; don't
Allow a single kiss!
If there's a kiss, I'll prove that I'm your lover:
I'll shout "That kiss is *mine!*"
And crush you in my arms.
But these are things that I can see. I fear
More blindly all the things
That clothing can conceal.
Don't press his leg with yours, touch thigh to thigh,
Or link his big hard foot
With your own dainty one.
I've done fresh things like that myself, and so
I have good reason for
My miserable fears.
Often, my girl and I have rushed our pleasure,
And finished the sweet job
Under a covering dress.
I trust you won't do that, but so you won't
Appear to, throw off that
Conspiratorial cloak.
Keep urging him to drink—but please don't kiss
Him while you beg—and while
He drinks, add more pure wine
Without his notice. If he passes out

Done in by sleep and wine,
Then we can plan, if place
And circumstance allow us. But when you
Get up to leave, and all
Of us are leaving, too,
Lose yourself in the middle of the crowd;
You'll find me in the crush
Or I'll find you; we'll touch.
But, damn, my words will help an hour or two
At most; the night commands
Us to be separate.
He'll lock you in at night, and I, in tears,
Follow as far as I'm
Allowed—to your rude doors.
He'll take his kisses, then not only kisses.
What you give me in secret,
You'll give him as his right,
Compelled. But act unwilling—yes, you can!—
And like a victim. Keep
Your pleasure silent; make
His Venus a grudging goddess. If my prayers
Are fully granted, he
Will have a wretched time.
Or second best, at least *you*'ll have no fun.
Whatever happens, though,
Tonight, please promise me
That you will say, tomorrow, when I ask,
That you refused him—and,
Say it convincingly!

1.5

The day was hot, the hour a bit past noon;
I lay upon my bed
To give myself a rest.
The shutters were half-open and half-closed,
So that the filtered light
Was forestlike, as when
Luminous twilight spreads as Phoebus leaves,
Or when the night has gone
But day is not yet born.
Such light is suitable for moral girls
Whose frightened modesty
Hopes for a hiding-place . . .

But look! Corinna's here, wrapped in a loose
Tunic, hair tumbling down
Both sides of her white neck,
Seductive as renowned Semiramis[2]
Upon her wedding night,
Or Laïs, loved by many.[3]
I snatched her dress, transparent though it was
And not much in the way,
But still, she fought for cover.
The battle thus went on: she lacked the will
To win, betrayed her cause,
And I won, handily.
She stood before my eyes, all clothing gone;
Her body had no fault
At all that I could see.
What shoulders and what arms I saw—and touched,
What breasts—how suitable
For squeezing, in their shape—
How flat the belly under her slim chest,
How large, how lush her hips,
How firm and young her thighs,
But why tell all the details? What I saw
Was perfect; we embraced
Body to body, bare.
You know the rest, I think; tired out, we slept.
I wish more noons like *that*
Would often come my way!

1.14

I used to say, "Stop doctoring your hair!"
Well, now it's happened, dear:
You have no hair to dye.
If you had left your hair alone, whose would
Be more luxuriant?
It reached right to your backside,
So fine you hesitated to arrange it,
Fine as the filmy robes
The darkskinned Seres wear,[4]
Fine as that thread the spider's slender foot

2. Semiramis—legendary queen of Assyria, who built the city of Babylon.
3. Laïs—famous Corinthian hetaira (courtesan).
4. Seres—the Chinese.

Pulls as he weaves his light
Work on the empty beam.
It wasn't black, nor was it gold, but rather
A mixture of the two;
Such color can be seen
Where in steep Ida's humid valleys, tall
Cedars stand, stripped of bark.
And it was docile hair, and suited to
A hundred styles, and never
Caused you a bit of pain.
The hairpin never broke it, nor the comb;
The slave who fixed your hair
Was safe from punishment;
I've often watched her styling it, and never
Observed a hairpin snatched
To jab the poor girl's arm.
I've often seen you with your hair not yet
Arranged, lie lounging on
Your crimson couch at dawn,
Well dressed in your disorder, as a Thracian
Bacchant, lying exhausted,
Careless on the green grass.
Yet that poor hair, so delicate, so downy,
Was tortured, made to suffer
So many evil things!
How patiently it gave itself to fire
And iron, to become
Twisted, tight-circling curls;
I cried out, "It's a crime, a crime to burn
That hair! It's beautiful
Just as it is: Oh, spare
That head, you iron woman! Away, away
With violence! Such hair
Ought not to burn, for it
Could teach your hairpins how fine hair should look!"
That lovely hair is dead,
So lovely that Apollo
Or Bacchus might have wished it for their own;
I could compare it with
The locks that nude Dione
Was painted holding up with dripping hands.
Why, now, do you complain
Of having lost that hair
You treated so severely? Silly girl,
Why do you put aside

Your mirror with such sorrow?
You see yourself with unfamiliar eyes;
To like what you see, forget
The self you used to see.
No tart's enchanted herbs have brought you harm;
No aged witch has washed
Your hair with water from
Haemonia; no disease (knock wood!) attacked you;
No jealous curses thinned
Your long, abundant hair;
Your loss was all your fault: you mixed and poured
With your own hands the poison
Given to your poor head.
Now captured Germany will send you hair;
Your looks will be the gift
Of a race we triumph over.
If a man admires your hair, you'll blush and say
"My beauty is store-bought;
Rather than praising me,
He's praising some Sygambrian! But I
Remember when my fame
Was genuinely mine."
Poor thing! She scarcely can hold back her tears,
And with her hands she hides
Her unrouged cheeks, dyed red
With shame, and fondles on her lap those curls
Which in old days were hers,
Which ought not to lie there.
Compose your face and pull yourself together:
The loss can be restored;
Your hair will grow again.

2.13

Reckless Corinna, having destroyed the burden
Of her full womb, lies sick,
In danger of her life.
She took this terrible risk without my knowledge;
I should be angry, but
Fear conquers any anger.
And yet, I either was the father, or,
I *think* so; what could be
Seems close enough to fact . . .

O Isis, lady of Paraetonium,[5]
And of Canopus' fertile
Fields, of Memphis, and
Palm-bearing Pharos, where the rushing Nile
Flows down in his broad channel
And glides through seven gates
Into the sea, I call you, by your sistra,
By the face of the holy one
Anubis, by your faithful
Osiris—may he always love your rites!
May lazy serpents slide
Around your altar gifts!
May horned Apis walk in your procession!
O turn your face this way
And spare two lives in one:
If you save my mistress, she'll give life to me.
Often she sits and serves
You, on your holy days,
At the shrine where Gallic horsemen brush your laurels.

And you who pity women
Who suffer in their wombs,
When hidden burdens stretch their bodies, late
In labor: Ilithyia,[6]
Be gentle, hear my prayers.
Care for her; she is worthy of your help.
And I myself will wear
White garments, and bring incense
To your smoking altars; I myself will place
At your feet the votive gifts
Inscribed by me, and saying
"From Naso, for Corinna's life," but you,
Goddess, must earn the gifts,
And justify the words.

Now you, Corinna, if it's right to scold you
At such a time, please let
This crisis be your last one!

5. Isis—the Egyptian fertility goddess. She was much worshiped by women, particularly courtesans, at Rome. Anubis was another Egyptian deity, with a dog's head (here presented as Isis's "faithful" pet); Osiris was Isis's lover. Apis was a sacred calf.
6. Ilithyia—goddess of childbirth.

3.4

You waste your time, grim husband, keeping guards
On your young wife: her will
Alone can do that job.
A wife who's chaste with fear removed, *is* chaste,
She who is pure because
She must be, isn't pure.
Although you keep her body safe, her mind's
A whore: you cannot jail
The wishes of the mind.
In fact, you cannot guard her body, either;
Lock every door? she'll find
Lovers inside the house.
Those who are free to wander, wander less;
The seeds of wickedness
Grow lazier, with power.
Trust me: your veto makes her lustier,
Indulge her, and you'll find
You're likelier to win.
Quite recently, I saw a horse run wild,
Like lightning, with the bit
Clamped in his stubborn teeth,
But when he felt the bridle lying slack
Upon his flying mane
And the reins loose, he stopped.
We seek forbidden things, pursue what's not
Allowed; the sick man lusts
For interdicted drinks.
The guard of Io had a hundred eyes[7]
In front, the same behind;
One Love deceived them all.
The tower of lasting rock and iron, where
The virgin Danaë[8]
Was locked, saw her give birth.
And yet Penelope, without a guard,[9]
With crowds of suitors, still
Remained inviolate.
What's guarded gains in value; extra locks
Are signals to the thief;

7. Guard of Io—Argus. See "Propertius," fn. 3.
8. Danaë—was locked in a tower. Zeus came to her as a shower of gold, and
she became, by him, the mother of the hero Perseus.
9. Penelope—the faithful wife of Odysseus.

Few men love what is free.
Men are attracted, not by your wife's face
But by your jealousy;
That shows she's worth a try.
Guarding makes her not pure, but dear to lovers
Her very fear, and not
Her body, boosts the price.
Be as angry as you like: forbidden fun
Is sweet; she's pleasing who
Can whisper, "I'm so scared!"
Also, it's *wrong* to keep a freeborn girl
In custody; that fear
Belongs to foreign slaves.
Do you want her pure just so her guard, a slave,
Can say "*I* kept her pure!"
And earn himself some praise?
Only a hick is wounded by his wife's
Affairs; he doesn't know
The customs of this town
In which the bastard sons of Mars were born,
Remus the child of Ilia,
And Ilia's Romulus.
Why choose a pretty wife, if only a faithful
One will please? The two
Do not occur combined.
Be smart: indulge your mistress; cancel that
Self-righteous face, and stop
Insisting on your Rights;
If you entertain the many friends your wife
Brings home, you'll easily
Become quite popular,
Much in demand at parties with the young,
And there'll be lots of gifts
You never bought, at home!

METAMORPHOSES 3.339–510
("ECHO AND NARCISSUS")

Throughout the Aonian towns, Tiresias
340 Grew famous for his flawless prophecies,
Given to all who asked. The first to test
The seer's veracity was a water nymph
Liriope, whom once the river-god
Cephisus caught, entwined in his meanders,
And under the waves he raped her. When her womb
Was ripe, the beautiful nymph brought forth her baby,
345 Already lovable, and named the boy
Narcissus, and she asked the seer if he
Would live to see old age. The prophet said
"Yes, if he never comes to know himself."
The prophecy seemed senseless, for some time,
350 Until his death and the manner of his dying
And his novel madness proved that it was true.

The son of the river-god was just sixteen,
Half-boy, half-man. Many girls wanted him
And many young men, but though his body still
Was young and soft, his mind was hard and haughty:
355 No girl or boy could touch him. Then one day
When he was driving stags into a net
A nymph named Echo saw him—she who could
Not stop herself from speaking, but could never
Be first to speak. She had a body, then:
She wasn't just a voice, but then as now
360 The garrulous girl could utter nothing but
The last words of a speech. The cause of this
Was Juno. Many times that goddess might
Have caught her husband Jove with one of the nymphs
In the mountains, making love, except that Echo
Cleverly kept her talking long enough
365 To let the nymphs escape. Saturnia[10]
Found out the truth, and said "That tongue of yours
Which cheated me, will lose its power now,
That voice be little use to you." Her threats
Were carried out: at the ends of speeches only
She duplicates the voice, and utters back
Only the words she hears.

10. Saturnia—another name for Juno.

She saw Narcissus

370 Wandering through the lonely countryside
And burned for him. Then, furtively, she followed
His tracks. The more she followed, all the more
Hotly her fire began to glow, as when
The eager sulphur smeared around a torch
Approaches flame and snatches it, and blazes.

375 How many times she wanted to approach him
With tender words, or plead seductively!
Her nature, conquering her, would not allow
Her to initiate, but she was ready
For what it would allow: some word from him
Which she might answer back in her own voice.
One day by chance the boy was separated
From his group of constant friends, and so he called,

380 "Is anyone here?" and Echo answered, "Here!"
Astonished, he looks all around, and shouts
In a louder voice, "Come here!" She calls the same
To the caller; he looks back, and seeing no one,
Says, "Why do you run away?" and gets for answer

385 The question that he asked. He stops, deceived
About what lies behind the other voice,
And says, "I'll stay here; you should come to me."
The perfect words for Echo: "Come to me!"
She answers, and, to make the words come true,
Pops out of the woods, and tries to throw her arms
Around his tempting neck. He darts away,

390 And running, cries out "Get away; I'll die
Before I'll let you touch my body!" She
Can only say "I'll let you touch my body!"

So spurned, she hides in the woods; humiliated,
She shields her face with boughs, and goes to live
In lonely caves, away from him. But love

395 Sticks with her, and her grief at his rejection
Grows worse; unsleeping sorrows wear away
Her suffering flesh; starvation shrivels up
Her skin; her body's moisture blows away;
Only a voice and bones remain, and then,
Only a voice: the bones are turned to stone.

400 And still she hides in the woods, and is not seen
In the hills, but she is heard by everyone—
Only a sound lives on in her, forever.

In the same way, Narcissus mocked the hopes
Of others, nymphs of the mountains and the waves,
And young men, too, his boyhood friends, until
One youth, humiliated, raised his hands
405 To heaven, praying, "May Narcissus love
As I have loved, and fail as I have failed!"
Nemesis heard, approving his just prayer.[11]

There was a pool, unmuddied, silvery
With shining water; shepherds never came
To drink there, nor the goats that grazed upon
410 The hills, nor any sheep. No bird or beast
Or falling tree branch ever troubled it.
Grass, made lush by the moisture, grew around it;
The woods let no sun in to warm its waters.
Here the boy came, tired out from hunting, hot,
And lay down, drawn by the water and the charm
415 Of the place. Before his thirst is eased, another
Thirst arises; captured by the image
He sees, he drinks, and falls in love with a thought
Which has no body; what he thinks is body
Is only water. Here he sticks, as if
He were a statue made from Parian marble.
420 Prone on the ground, he stares at those twin stars
—His eyes—and ringlets worthy of Apollo
Or Bacchus, his smooth cheeks and ivory neck,
His well-shaped mouth, his snowy skin, just touched
With tints of rose; he looks with wonder on
Those qualities that make him wonderful.
425 He loves himself, the fool; as he admires,
He is himself admired, and as he seeks,
Is sought; he is the one who lights the fire
And at the same time burns. How many times
He tries in vain to kiss the cheating water!
How often, aching for the neck he sees,
He thrusts his arms down in the pool, but never
430 Can catch himself with them! He doesn't know
What he is seeing, but the sight inflames
The one who sees: the eyes that lie to him
Themselves are mocked and lied to. Gullible boy,
Why do you long, in vain, for passing pictures?
The thing you seek is nowhere; what you love—

11. Nemesis—goddess of vengeance.

Just turn—you will destroy it. You are seeing
The shadow, only, of a reflected image.
435 It's nothing in itself; it comes with you
And stays and leaves with you—if you can leave.

No need for food or sleep can drag him away;
He lies on the shady grass, and gazes at
The fraudulent form, his eyes unsatisfied.
440 Those eyes are killing him; he lifts himself
A little, and extending his arms toward
The trees that stand as witnesses, he cries,
"You forest! Has there ever been a love
So cruel? You have seen; your shadows give
A hiding-place to many lovers. Tell me,
In your long years, your centuries of life,
445 Has anyone so suffered as I do?
I see, I love, but what I love and see
I cannot find; confusion spoils my love.
No ocean separates us, no long roads,
No mountains, and no fortress with locked gates,
I suffer all the more; we are divided
450 By just a little water! He himself
Wants to be held! As often as I try,
Through the clear water, to give him a kiss
I see his supine lips strain up to meet me;
You'd think that we could touch, so little stands
Between us. You, whoever you are, come out!
There's no one else like you; why do you tease me?
455 Where do you go, when I reach for you? I think
It cannot be my age or looks which drive
You off, for nymphs have been in love with me.
You offer me some hope with your loving gaze;
I reach my arms out to you, you reach yours;
I smile, and you smile back; I've seen your tears
460 When I was crying; if I nod, you nod;
I speak; your lovely lips are moving, too,
But what you say can never reach my ears . . .

"Oh, no! He is myself! I understand;
My image doesn't fool me now. I burn
For love of me; I kindle and bear the flames.
465 What shall I do? Be asked, or ask? Indeed—
What can I ask for? What I want is mine:

My wealth has made me poor; I wish I could
Withdraw from my own body. Here's a novel
Prayer for a lover: may the one I love
Depart! Now sorrow weakens me; I have
470 Not long to live; I shall be snuffed out young.
Death is no heavy burden; death will take
My grief away. I only wish that he,
My darling, could survive—but now we die,
Two loving friends united in one soul."

He spoke, and in his madness he returned
475 To gazing at the face. His tears disturbed
The water, and the picture in the pool,
Stirred up, grew indistinct. He saw it leaving,
And shouted, "Where are you running? Stay, do not
Desert your lover, cruel boy! At least,
Though touching is forbidden, let me look,
And feed my wretched madness with your face!"
480 Weeping, he ripped his tunic, and he pounded
His naked chest with fists as white as marble.
The beating gave his chest a rosy blush
Much like the color of an apple, partly
Rosy and partly white, or like the red
485 On young grapes, ripening. He saw himself
As the water cleared again, and could not bear it.
As golden wax is melted by a flame,
Or frost in the morning by the warming sun,
490 Wasted by love, he melts, consumed by the hidden
Fire, little by little. Now no trace
Remains of the rosy color or the whiteness,
No liveliness, no strength, no more of those
Good looks which pleased so lately, no more body
Which Echo once had loved. But when she saw this,
Although still angry and remembering,
495 She wept, and every time the wretched boy
Cried out in pain, her voice gave back the cry.
And when he beat his breast in sorrow, she
Returned the sounds of mourning. When at last,
Still staring at the pool, he said, "Poor boy,
500 I loved you, but in vain," all of his words
Came back again, and when it was the end,
"Goodbye," he said, and Echo said "Goodbye."
He laid his weary head on the green grass;
Death closed the eyes that loved their master's beauty.

The underworld received him; now he gazes
505 At Stygian water. But his Naiad sisters
   Wept and cut locks of hair for their dear brother,
   And Dryads mourned, and Echo joined their mourning.
   They made a funeral pyre and bier, and carried
   Torches to shake, but could not find his body;
   They found, instead, a little yellow flower,
510 With petals of pure white around the center.

POETS OF THE
SILVER
AGE

MARTIAL

M. Valerius Martialis was born at Bilbilis in Spain, in about A.D. 40. In 64, he immigrated to Rome, where he spent most of his life as a popular versifier; in all he produced at least twelve volumes of mostly brief poems. He made friends with the literary lights of the period—his fellow Spaniards and first patrons Seneca and Lucan and, later, Juvenal and Pliny the Younger—and was honored by several emperors. He did moderately well for himself, earning the title *eques* ("knight"), as well as a small farm and a house in Rome; his poems, however, are filled with complaints about his poverty. In his last years he retired to Bilbilis, where he died in about 104.

It is almost impossible to anthologize Martial without making his work seem far more wonderful than it really is. For one thing, he is easy to translate: his pithy, pointed, self-contained epigrams fit nicely into English forms of rhymed light verse. And, at his best, Martial is brilliant; his choicest verses present us not only with a lively panorama of Roman social life under the early empire but also with a memorable array of sharp, nasty, funny, racy, occasionally wise observations about recognizably human individuals: quacks, climbers, incompetents, moneygrubbers, professional virgins, professional nonvirgins, self-important intellectuals, drunks, prigs, penny pinchers, pinchers of backsides and kissers of the same.

But his humor is often cruel or unfair: he picks on deformity, ugliness, old age, disease, poverty, and lower-class origins; he is particularly unpleasant to women. He never picks on the truly powerful; he is at his most loathesome in his cringing flattery of the emperor Domitian, who was not really a nice man. He is perhaps the most obscene of the Roman poets—and it was not a literary tradition noted for chaste delicacy of expression—but there is little fun in his filth, which often amounts to little more than catalogues of the usual "unusual" practices. If there is humor in it, it is essentially the simple humor of the five-year-old who can go into paroxysms of laughter at the mere pronunciation, *out loud*, of a word like "underpants" or "wee-wee." Aside from the merely dirty, the toadying, and the tastelessly cruel, many of Martial's epigrams are simply dull: perhaps time has blunted their point, or maybe—it seems likely—some of them never had much cutting power to begin with.

But, after all, there are twelve volumes to choose from. I have not chosen to give the reader a really representative sampling of Martial at his most tedious or embarrassing or pointless. I hope the reader will be forgiving and enjoy what's here.

EPIGRAMS

1.16

Some lines in here are good, some fair,
And most are frankly rotten;
No other kind of book, Avitus,[1]
Can ever be begotten.

1.18

What ails you, Tucca, that you mix
In with your old and fine
Falernian, those musty dregs
Of awful Vatican wine?
Did the priceless wine mistreat you once?
What harm did it ever do
To merit this? Or the other stuff,
Does it have some hold on you?
Forget your Roman guests; it is
A heinous crime to throttle
A Falernian, or give strong poison
To a Campanian—bottle.
No doubt your drinking-friends deserved
To die in deadly pain;
That precious amphora should not
Have been so foully slain.

1.28

It's slander to say Acerra stinks
Of last night's wine. To tell
The truth, he drinks till dawn, and so
That's nice fresh booze you smell!

1. Avitus—it is not necessary to know who Avitus was, or Tucca, or any of
the men and women addressed in Martial's poems. In most cases, no person
alive knows who they were.

1.37

To Bassus:
You relieve yourself in a golden urn
(Poor urn!) and think it's fine,
But you drink from glass. I guess your shit
Is dearer than your wine.

1.38

To Fidentinus:
That verse is mine, you know, which you're
Reciting. But you quote it
So execrably, that I think
I'll let you say *you* wrote it.

1.47

Doctor Diaulus has changed his trade:
He now is a mortician,
With the same results he got before
As a practicing physician.

1.71

I've drunk six toasts to you, Laevia; come to me!
And seven for Justina—Come to me!
Now five for Lycas, four for Lyde; come!
And three for Ida; now I've numbered all
My girl friends in Falernian, and none
Has come. One more, for Somnus: *he* will come.[2]

1.83

To Manneia:
Your doggie licks your face and lips: how *sweet*!
No wonder—*you* know what dogs like to eat.

2. Somnus—the god of Sleep.

2.12

To Postumus:
Your kisses smell of myrrh; you always wear
Exotic odors, musk or sandalwood
Or something. I suspect a man who always
Smells so sweet: he must not smell too good.

2.89

Gaurus, you have a fault for which
I freely pardon you:
You love to drink too much, too late;
That vice was Cato's, too.[3]
I'll even praise your scribbling
Verses, instead of prose,
With NO help from the Muses, for
That fault was Cicero's.
You vomit: so did Antony,
You squander: records *may* show
Apicius as your model—now,
Who led you to fellatio?

3.68

Madam: my little book, so far,
In its entirety
Up to this point, has been for you;
From now on, it's for me.
The gym, the locker room, the baths
Are next; you'd better skip
This part and go away, my dear,
The men are going to strip.
Terpsichore is staggering
From all the wine and roses,

---

3. Cato—either Cato the Elder (234–149 B.C.), a stern moralist but author of a collection of jokes, among other things, or Cato the Younger (95–46 B.C.), another upright citizen, who opposed Julius Caesar. Cicero was the famous statesman of the first century B.C.; Antony the opponent of Octavian (Augustus); Apicius a gourmet and author of the Augustan period. All, in other words, eminent models "from the history books."

She lays aside her shame and starts
Assuming naughty poses,
In no ambiguous terms she names
Quite openly, that Thing
Which haughty Venus welcomes
In the rituals, in spring,
That thing which stands in gardens
Scaring thieves with its great size,
Which virgins peek at modestly
With almost-covered eyes.
I know you, Madam: you were tired
And just about to quit
My lengthy little book; *Now* you'll
Devour all of it!

3.87

To Chione:
Rumor has it your twat is pure
As snow, and you've never screwed;
But nonetheless when you take a bath
You won't go in the nude.
You're acting very foolish
If you really fear disgrace,
If you're so modest, take your pants
And cover up that face!

4.38

That's right, Galla, say no to me—
Frustrated lust grows stronger
While satisfaction cloys. But, Galla,
Don't say no much longer!

4.56

To Gargilianus:
You want me to call you *generous*
Because you shower gold
On widows, and send costly gifts
To none but the very old?

There's nothing quite so nasty
Or so sordidly unpleasant
As what you do and what you say
When you call a snare a "present."
The treacherous hook is "generous"
To the greedy fishes, too;
Trappers lay bait for stupid beasts—
They're generous just like you.
You want to learn the meaning of
True generosity?
I'll teach you about pure largesse:
Just send your gifts to me!

5.10

"Why is it that the living win
So little fame or praise?
And why do readers not admire
The work of their own days?"

Well, Regulus, it is the way
Of human jealousy;
Men always loathe all modern things
And love antiquity.
We seek the ancient shade of Pompey's
Ugly portico,
And praise the temple of Catullus:
We love its crudeness so!
O Rome: you read old Ennius
Though Virgil's works survive;
They say that even Homer was
Ridiculed while alive;
Laureled Menander rarely had
Much honor given to him,
And as for Ovid, in his day
Only Corinna knew him.

But you, my little books, don't rush
To win me a great name,
If only death brings praise, I'm in
No hurry for that fame!

5.43

Laecania has white teeth and Thais
Black, but you may stop
Wondering: Laecania's
Were purchased in a shop.

5.76

King Mithridates often drank
Some poison, to protect
Himself from plots. That way, no toxic
Drugs could have effect.

You, Cinna, spend so little on
Your food, it would appear
You've made yourself immune, in case
There's ever a famine here!

7.3

To Pontilianus:
You ask me why I don't send you
My books of poetry?
The answer is I'm terrified
You'll send *your* verse to *me*!

7.53

To Umber:
Last Saturnalia, friend, I think[4]
You must have passed along
To me each little gift you got
Yourself; now am I wrong?
Twelve tablets, seven toothpicks came;
Sponge, napkin, cup; not far
Behind, a half a peck of beans
Some olives, a black jar
Of cheap new wine, some withered prunes
Some figlets (not too big)

4. Saturnalia—the Roman midwinter festival, much like Christmas.

And a monstrous heavy urn, filled up
With the other kind of fig.
I'd say these gifts, in all, were worth
Thirty sesterces or less,
But eight huge Syrian slaves were needed
To carry the whole mess.

I have a better plan: next year
When you're sending gifts to me
You'll find one boy could tote five pounds
Of silver easily!

7.83

That barber's careful; his customer's
The hairiest of men;
By the time he trims the sideburns
The beard has grown again.

8.66

To Gallicus:
"Please, Marcus, tell the *truth*," you say,
"That's all I want to hear!"
If you read a poem or plead a case
You din it in my ear:
"The truth, the honest truth!" you beg,
It's damned hard to deny
Such a request. So here's the truth:
You'd rather have me lie.

10.65

Since you, Charmenion, come from Corinth
And I from quite another
Part of the world, from Tagus, tell m
Why do you call me "brother"?

You're Greek—my ancestors were Celts
And Spaniards. Do we share
Some physical resemblances?
Well, you have oily hair,

In ringlets—my stiff Spanish locks
Are obstinately straight;
I'm shaggy-legged and bristle-cheeked—
Daily you depilate

Your silky skin. Your voice is light;
You lisp in a charming way—
My voice, as my loins can teste-fy,
Is gruff. And so I'll say:

We're less alike than eagles and doves,
Or lions and does, so Mister,
Don't you call me "brother," or
I'll have to call you "sister."

11.47

Does Lattara shun the baths where crowds
Of women go? It's true.
And why is he so particular?
—He does not wish to screw.

He never goes to Pompey's Porch
As many others do,
Or Isis' shrine, where whores hang out,
—He does not wish to screw.

Why does he take those long cold baths
Anointed with Spartan goo,
In the waters of the Virgin? Why?
—He does not wish to screw.

If he's so scared of women
(That contaminating crew)
Why is he fond of cunnilingus?
—He does not wish to screw.

11.93

Flames have gutted th'abode Pierian
Of the wide-renownèd poet Theodorus,
Didst thou permit this sacrilege, Apollo?
Where were ye, Muses' Chorus?

Ay me, I fondly sigh, that was a crime
A wicked deed, a miserable disaster,
Ye Gods are much to blame: ye burnt the house
But failed to singe its master!

12.56

Poor Polycharmus, you're always sick,
Ten times a year, or more,
It hurts us more than it does you
In fact, it's an awful bore
Always giving you get-well gifts,[5]
Now, here's what should be done:
We're sick of your sicknesses, my friend,
Let this be your *final* one!

5. Actually, in Rome such gifts were given after the patient recovered—so to speak, "got-well" gifts.

JUVENAL

One more time, it is necessary to say that few certain facts are known about the poet's life. D. Junius Juvenalis was probably born at Aquinum, a town not far from Rome, perhaps in about A.D. 60. He may have been in the army; he may have been in Britain and perhaps in Egypt. Probably he lived most of his life in Rome. At one point in his life he may have been exiled for a time, perhaps because of a satirical attack on an actor-favorite of one of the emperors. He lived a fairly long life, until at least 128. His extant work consists of sixteen satires written in dactylic hexameter, issued at different times, in five books or collections.

Juvenal's satires are often contrasted with those of Horace (see "Horace," Satire 1.9 ["The Bore"]). In these comparisons, Horace is usually called "gentle," "leisurely," "amusing," "urbane," "tolerant," and "polished," and is said to aim his "kindly" darts at "folly." Juvenal, on the other hand, attracts words like "savage," "one-sided," "bitter," and "darkly pessimistic," and his "scathing attacks" are directed at "vice." This generalization is, predictably, generally valid. Juvenal's works are full of anger and bitterness, against bad poets, bad emperors, bad philosophers, homosexuals, women, Greeks, Jews, athletes, soldiers, actors, patrons, clients, toadies, crooks, and above all, The Rich. He is an attacker, of unequaled vividness and violence. His targets are presented specifically, concretely, realistically. He doesn't waste words. He is not "leisurely," as Horace is, and consequently he is seldom boring, as Horace (it must be admitted) often is. But those who see only Juvenal's dark side, and who deny him humor, ought to have their funny bones examined.

True, it is impossible to make anyone laugh by pointing out what makes *us* laugh. But consider a few of Juvenal's nice touches. Satire 1 has the subject, "why do I write satire?" The poet describes a few of the flamboyantly rotten characters of his society and concludes that in such times the difficulty is not in writing satire—it's just about impossible *not* to write it! Then, there is the Satire 6, a nasty attack on women in general, which in fact provides us with our best evidence that there was some sort of women's movement in the first century A.D. The poet lets us know that he is not really *quite* so deadly serious as he seems, when he comes to that *rara avis*, the Totally Good Woman—and says, well, she'd be worse than any of the others: She'd make *you* look bad by contrast! One further example: In the satire presented in this book, Juvenal presents us with a criminal, one of the muggers who made the streets of Rome so terrifying at night (and so cozily familiar to the readers of Dr. Johnson's *London* or today's *New York Times*). The crook is having trouble getting to sleep, says Juvenal, because he happens not to have killed anybody today. "Grim hyperbole," says one reader. "Awful; almost true; *funny*" says another.

Much of Juvenal's work is not humorous, of course. The great *Satire* 10 (which Johnson adapted as *The Vanity of Human Wishes*) is almost wholly serious. But readers who insist on seeing only savagery and darkness in Juvenal are in danger of as much one-sidedness as they impute to the poet.

Juvenal's villain in the satire presented here is The City. Readers will find some unfamiliar terrain, like the strange and burdensome custom of the morning visit (*salutatio*) that every "client" was expected to pay on his patron. Nearly every Roman was someone's client, or dependent, and was expected to greet his patron every morning and to support him in any way he could, for example by voting for him in elections. The patron, in turn, gave his clients occasional help (for example, legal assistance), and was expected to give each morning visitor a gift of food. Many patrons were themselves clients, of more powerful citizens. This complex network of dependent relationships had probably been useful in the early days of Rome, but by Juvenal's time it had become a humiliating waste of time. There are other aspects of Juvenal's Rome (for example, slavery) that we find unfamiliar; but generally, the appalling and amusing thing about this ancient city is that its miseries and dangers are so recognizable. Catullus, Propertius, Ovid, gave us a glimpse into the fun, excitement and glamor of the eternal city; but we must be grateful to Juvenal, too, for letting us see the seamy side of the Grandeur that was Rome.

SATIRE 3 ("THE CITY OF ROME")

I am upset: my old friend's leaving Rome.
But still, I praise his choice, to settle down
At Cumae, and to give one citizen,
At least, to the old Sibyl. There, he'll find [1]
The gateway, not to hell, but to the beach,
A nice retreat beside the pleasant shore.
I'd even like *Prochyta* better than [2]
The crowded streets of Rome. What desert isle
Could be so nasty or so desolate
That you'd prefer to shudder, here in Rome
At buildings crashing down, and spreading fires,
The thousand dangers of this violent town
And poets reciting in the *summer*time?

My friend stood silent, watching his entire
Household being assembled in one cart
Under that ancient arch, where the aqueduct
Built overhead, drips down upon the road.
Here good King Numa nightly came to terms
With his lady friend, but nowadays the grove, [3]
With its holy spring and shrine, is rented out
To Jews, who own a basket and some hay
For all their furniture. Now, every tree
Must pay the people rent for its own space,
The Muses are evicted, and the woods
Are beggars. We go down, my friend and I,
Into Egeria's valley and the caves
"Restored" so falsely. How much closer we
Might feel the Water Spirit, if her spring
Had real green grass around its edge, and no
Marble insulting the plain Italian rock!

Here, then, Umbricius said, "Since there's no place
In town for honest men, and no reward
For labor—since today, I have less cash
Than yesterday; Tomorrow will rub off
A bit more from that little bit I have—

1. Sibyl—see "Virgil," fn. 4.
2. Prochyta—a small island off Campania.
3. Lady friend—the nymph Egeria, who taught the legendary Roman king all about religion.

I'm going to that place where Daedalus[4]
Took off his weary wings, while my white hair
Is new to me, and my old age still young
Standing upright, while the Fates have still
Some time to spin for me, and while I can
Still walk on both my feet without a cane.

I hereby do yield up my fatherland:
Let Catulus live there, Artorius,
All those who can convert black trades to white:
The contractors (in temples, bridges, dams)
The sewer scrubbers, funeral managers,
All those who aren't too proud to sell themselves.
Those men who used to blow the horn at shows,
Perpetual hangers-on, whose puffed-out cheeks
Were known throughout the boondocks, now themselves
Produce the shows, and, as the crowd desires,
Turn up their thumbs and kill, and win applause.
Now they are back, contracting to erect
The public urinals; why shouldn't they?
They can do anything, those lucky souls
Whom Fortune raises from a lowly state
Up to the rooftops, when She wants a laugh.
What could I do at Rome? I cannot lie;
I cannot praise a wretched book, or beg
To have a copy; I am ignorant
Of what the Stars predict; I won't and can't
Promise a father's funeral to his son;
I've never learned what frog entrails might mean;
Others are better go-betweens, to take
A lover's words and presents to a bride.
I cannot be accomplice to a thief,
And so no governor wants me on his staff;
I'm crippled, like a body without arms.

Who's counted as a friend these days, unless
He shares a guilty secret, and his soul
Simmers with facts too hot to be disclosed?
That man who's whispered something innocent
To you—he doesn't owe you anything.
That man is Verres' pet who, any time

4. Daedalus—the mythical Greek inventor (father of Icarus; see "Horace," fn. 9).

He wants to, can have Verres brought to trial.
My friend, don't place so high a value on
The sand that shady Tagus washes down
And rolls into the sea, with all its gold,
That you lose sleep for it, or take a bribe
You must repay some day, regretfully,
Or be your mighty patron's constant fear.

"One race is now most pleasing to the rich,
A race which I detest; I'm not ashamed
To name them; no, I'm eager to admit,
My fellow Romans, that I cannot stand
Any Greek city—tell me, what percent
Of Rome's worst dregs come from Achaean shores?
The Syrian Orontes long ago
Flowed down into the Tiber, carrying
Its foreign lingo, immorality,
Flute girls, sambucas, barbarous kettledrums,
And whores who work the Circus. Go there, look,
If turbaned foreign bitches turn you on!
"Your average Roman hick now dresses in
A 'trechedipna,' and adorns himself
With 'niceterian' ornaments around
His 'ceromatically' anointed neck.[5]
This Greek's from hilly Sicyon, and that
From Amydon, or Andros, Tralles, or
Samos, or Alabanda; every one
Is seeking the exclusive Esquiline,
Or the hill which took its name from willow twigs,[6]
To become the vital organs of some house,
And later on, its master. Clever, quick,
Obnoxiously aggressive, eloquent,
With floods of words Isaeus couldn't match.
Now tell me, what do you think he is, that Greek?
He carries in him anyone you want:
Professor, orator, geometer,
A painter, wrestling coach, an acrobat
Who dances on the tightrope, sorcerer,
Doctor, or seer. The hungry little Greek
Knows everything; just point up at the skies,
And tell him 'Get there somehow'; off he flies!

5. Trechedipna, niceteria, ceroma—all Greek slang, meaning, roughly "run-to-dinner" (slippers, or a coat), "victory-award," "wrestlers' ointment."
6. Willow twigs—the Viminal.

(In short, that man who put on wings was not[7]
Sarmatian, Moor, or Thracian, but was born
In downtown Athens.) Come now, shouldn't I
Run from these purple-wearing people? See,
He signs his name before me, and reclines
On better furniture than I possess,
That man who blew in yesterday, on winds
That used to bring us plums and little figs.
Is it worth nothing that my infancy,
Nourished by Sabine berries, breathed the air
Upon the Aventine? Consider this:
This race of cunning flatterers will praise
The speech of an illiterate, the looks
Of one deformed from birth; they will compare
A weakling's scrawny neck to Hercules',
Straining to hold Antaeus off the ground,[8]
And marvel at a squeaky little voice
No better than the rooster's when he pecks
His mate. We, too, can praise these qualities,
But *they're* convincing. How those Greeks can act!
When one of them plays Thais, or a wife,
Or Doris, when she strips her pallium off,
You'd think it was a woman speaking, not
An actor in a mask, and you would swear
That nothing hung between his legs, except
A little crack—but back at home in Greece,
Antiochus is no celebrity,
Neither is Stratocles, Demetrius,
Or pansy Haemus: All of Hellas is
A stage, and every Greek's a player. Laugh,
He'll burst his sides with deafening guffaws,
But if he sees his friend has shed a tear,
He'll weep and never feel a bit of pain.
In wintertime, if someone lights a fire
He grabs his overcoat, but if you say
'I'm hot,' the fellow breaks into a sweat.
I can't compete with him. He's better off
Who can, at any time of night or day,
Take his expression from another's face,
And praise, and throw his hands up with delight,

7. Wings—Daedalus. See fn. 4 above.
8. Antaeus—a nasty giant, a wrestler who grew stronger every time he touched the Earth (his mother). Hercules defeated and killed him by holding him in the air.

If his friend belches loudly, pisses straight,
Or if his golden potty, when it's dumped,
Makes interesting noises. Furthermore,
There's nothing safe or sacred to his crotch;
He doesn't spare the matron of the house,
The virgin daughter, or her fiancé,
Nor yet the family's innocent young son;
If no one younger is available,
He'll lay the aged grandma of his friend.
Now, since I'm started on the Greeks, let's skip
The vices of their naked schools, and note
Crime of a heavier fabric: that old man,
That 'Stoic' who betrayed and killed his friend [9]
Barea, his disciple—he was raised
Upon the shore where Pegasus let drop
A feather. There's no place for Romans here
Where some Protogenes or Diphilus
Or some Hermarchus rules the house, and can,
Like all his race, not ever share a friend
But keeps him to himself. For when he drips
Into the willing ear a drop or two
Of poison from his country and himself
I'm exiled from the house, and all my years
Of servitude are lost: nowhere but Rome
Can clients be so easily tossed out.

"And Romans, too, must share the blame: what use,
What honor's left for poor men serving here?
You rise, punctiliously, before the dawn,
And, in your toga, run—only to see
The praetor, hurrying his lictor on,
Urging more speed, for fear his colleague might
Be first to greet those childless heiresses,
Modia and Albina, who have been
Awake for hours. Here in Rome the son
Of freeborn parents must give up his place
To any rich man's slave: for *he* can pay
A tribune's yearly wages, to enjoy
The charms of highborn Catiena or
Calvina, when the urge occurs, but *you*
Are doubtful, if some dressed-up hooker's face
(Chione's, for example) pleases you,

9. Stoic—Egnatius Celer, who gave false evidence against his former pupil
Barea Soranus in A.D. 66.

Uncertain if you can afford to bring
Her down from that high chair. In lawsuits, too,
Though you may bring a witness honorable
As Scipio, the host of Cybele,
Or good King Numa, or the man who saved
Trembling Minerva from the blazing shrine,[10]
Your morals are the *last* thing jurors want
To know; the first is always: is he rich?
How many slaves? How large an acreage?
How many serving-dishes does he own?
What *size* are they? A man's word is believed
Exactly in proportion to his cash.
Although he swears by all the altars of
Rome, or of Samothrace, the poor man's oath
Is nothing; they assume that he must care
Nothing for gods or thunderbolts, because
It's clear the gods are indifferent to *him*.
Then, too, the poor man's always offering
Occasion and material for jokes;
His overcoat is dirty, or it's torn,
His toga is a little less than white,
One of his shoes is gaping, where it's split,
His tunic shows some coarse, new thread: the scars
Of many a stitched-up wound. The hardest thing
To bear about unhappy poverty
Is that it makes the poor man *laughable*.

"Then, in the theatre: 'How *dare* you try
To sit here with the Knights? Aren't you ashamed?
You're *much* too poor—get up!' Of course. These seats
Are now reserved for sons of pimps, conceived
In brothels; here, the gladiator's boy
So nicely dressed, applauds, beside the sons
Of trainers, or of sweating auctioneers:
That was the will of silly Otho, who[11]
Put us in separate seats. What poor young man
Who couldn't match his girl friend's moneybags
Has ever been approved as son-in-law?
What poor man ever gets a legacy?
Or is appointed to an aedile's staff?

10. Man who saved Minerva—L. Caecilius Metellus, who in 241 B.C. rescued
a statue of Minerva from a fire.
11. Otho—Nero's successor; he was emperor for a very short time.

Rome's needy citizens should, long ago,
Have formed their ranks and marched right out of town.

"It isn't easy for a man to rise
When poverty obscures his talents; here,
It's harder still: it costs a fortune, here,
To rent a wretched living space; to fill
The bellies of your slaves, and buy yourself
A stingy little meal. You'd be ashamed
In Rome to eat from earthenware, but if
You were transported, suddenly, to dine
With Sabines or with Marsians, you'd forget
Such snobbery, contented in your coarse
Venetian cloak. Let us admit the truth:
In many parts of Italy, no one
Puts on a toga, till he is a corpse.
Even at festivals, when everyone
Is being rather grand—a popular
Farce is playing (again) upon the stage
Of the grassy theatre—some farmer's child
Shrieks in his mother's bosom, terrified
At the gaping, clay-white masks—there you will see
No difference in dress between the crowd
And the magistrates up front: even the proud
Aediles are quite contented, there, to cloak
In plain white tunics, their great dignity.
Here we all dress impeccably, and spend
More than we have; to look a bit more chic
We dip into some borrowed money box.
One vice is common to us all in Rome:
Our life is all pretentious poverty.

"In short, all things in Rome come at a price:
Tell me, what do you pay for the privilege
Of greeting Cossus—sometimes—at his house
Or getting one of Veiento's tight-lipped stares?
The first one asks you in to celebrate
His favorite slave's first beard—the other one
Invites you to observe *his* darling boy
Whose pretty curls are being cut today;
The house is full of cakes; you'll have to tip
The slaves for one; come, take it; let the crumbs
Leave you this bitter taste inside your mouth:
As clients—freemen—we pay tribute to
Augment the fortune of some well-dressed slave.

"What man who lives at cool Praeneste, or
Volsinii, among the shady hills,
Or simple Gabii, or on the slopes
Of Tibur, ever fears his house will fall?
But here we occupy a city propped
Mostly on slender reeds, for that is how
The rental agent keeps his tenements
From falling, while he patches up the wide
Cracks in the ancient walls, and orders you
To sleep securely, under the shaky roof.
Men should not have to live in places where
They are in constant fear of night and fires.
Ucalegon, downstairs, is shouting now [12]
For water, has already carried out
His few belongings—now the smoke begins
To fill your third-floor attic; you're the last
To know, since the alarm began below,
On the first floor, and who will be the last
To burn?—that man who's sheltered from the rain
Only by tiles, where pigeons lay their eggs.
Poor Codrus had a bed too little for
The midget Procula; for ornaments
He had six pottery jars, a drinking mug,
A Centaur kneeling under a marble slab,
And an old chest, which held some books in Greek
Whose godlike poems had been half-devoured
By barbarous Roman mice who knew no Greek.
Codrus had nothing; no one would deny
The statement; yet, unlucky Codrus lost
The nothing which was everything to him.
This is the crowning stone upon his pile
Of miseries: he's stripped of all, he begs
For crumbs, and now no one will ask him in
To share a meal, or spend a night or two.

"If Asturicus' mansion is destroyed,
Rome's matrons tear their hair, important men
Wear mourning, and the courts are ordered closed.
Then we lament the town's disasters; then
We declare war on Fire. The house is still
Smouldering, but already someone comes
To offer marble, and whatever things

12. Ucalegon—name of a Trojan, whose house burns in the *Aeneid* of Virgil.

Are needed for rebuilding; someone else
Gives gleaming naked statues, and a third
Pledges a Polycleitan masterpiece
Or one made by Euphranor, while a fourth[13]
Offers up ancient treasures from the shrines
Of Asia; someone else will donate books,
And bookshelves, with Minerva over them,
While yet another offers to provide
A bushel of silver plate. Why, Persicus
—Most sumptuous of heirless men in Rome—
After *his* fire, received such splendid stuff
By way of reparation that they say
(Not unsurprisingly) he *set* the fire.

"If you could bear to tear yourself away
From circuses, you'd find that you could buy
The finest house in Fabrateria
Or Sora or Frusino, for the price
You pay to *rent* a year of darkness, here.
You'd have a little garden and a well
Shallow enough to dip your bucket in
Quite easily, without a rope, to draw
Some water for your seedlings. There you'd live
With your darling hoe, and be the overseer
Of a well-worked plot, from which you could provide
A hundred Pythagoreans with a feast.[14]
To be an *owner*, in whatever place,
However far removed, is worth something—
Even if your domain would scarcely hold
A single lizard, yet it is your own.

"In Rome, insomnia kills off the sick,
Whose illnesses, to start with, were brought on
—Through lack of rest—by undigested food
Stuck in their burning stomachs. Tell me, what
Tenement takes in Somnus as a guest?[15]
Only the rich sleep well in Rome. And that's
The start of our disorder. When the carts
Rumble across the narrow, winding streets,
When the cattle drivers, blocked in traffic, curse,

13. Polycleitus, Euphranor—famous Greek sculptors.
14. Pythagoreans—a vegetarian sect.
15. Somnus—Sleep.

Sleep would be snatched even from Drusus, or [16]
A sea calf. When a rich man gets his call
To social duty, crowds give way; he glides
In his huge Liburnian car, above their heads,
And on the way, he reads, or writes, or naps
Inside; it's easy enough to sleep behind
The window of a litter, when it's shut.
And he'll arrive before us, too; my path
Is blocked, when I am hurrying, by the wave
Of those in front, while the great crowd behind
Squeezes my tail: one digs his elbows in,
Another knocks me with a heavy pole,
I get my head banged by a beam, and then
A metal tub; my legs are smeared with mud
And soon from every angle giant feet
Are trampling me; a soldier firmly plants
His hobnailed boot upon my little toe.

"See all the smoke? That crowd is going to
A potluck supper—there must be
A hundred guests, each with a portable
Stove full of food behind him: Corbulo [17]
Himself could hardly carry all the stuff—
Big pots and other things upon his head—
Which that poor little slave must tote along
With rigid neck, while, as he runs, he fans
The coals, and splits his tunic, newly patched.
Here comes a builder's wagon: in it, trembling,
A giant fir tree; in another cart
They're carrying a pine—they nod, on high,
Like gods, and threaten all the partygoers.
For, if that axle, carrying marble from
Liguria, should break and overturn
And pour its mountain down upon the crowd,
What body would be left intact? What limbs,
What bones could still be found? The pulverized
Cadavers of the masses disappear
Just like their souls. But meanwhile, safe at home,
The slaves are washing dishes, puffing up
The little fire; the glistening scrapers ring,
Towels and oil are laid out for the bath.
And, while they hurry, each one at his job,

16. Drusus—perhaps the emperor Claudius, who fell asleep all the time.
17. Corbulo—a general of the time of Nero, said to be gigantic.

Their master sits already on the bank,
A novice shade, and shudders when he sees
The hideous ferryman. He cannot hope,[18]
Unlucky man, to cross the filthy flood:
No penny's in his mouth to pay the fare.

"Now, think of the various dangers of the night:
How high the roof from which a tile falls down
And hits your head—how often cracked or smashed
Pots tumble out the windows—with what force
They smash and chip the paving stones below!
You'd be considered rash and negligent
If you went out to dinner without first
Making a will—so many forms of death
Wait for you in the open windows, when
You pass below, at night. You'd better pray
A silent prayer for mercy, that they'll be
Content to dump their chamber pots on you.

"The drunken thug, who happens to have missed
Killing a man tonight, is lying awake
Much like Achilles when he mourned his friend,
Tossing and turning, first supine, then prone;
Only a brawl will help him get to sleep.
But still, however rash and young he feels,
However hot with wine, he'll take some care
Not to molest that man whose scarlet cloak
And throng of bodyguards, and mass of lights,
And bronze oil lamps warn him to keep away.
My escort is the moon, or the faint glow
Of a candle—and I'm frugal with the wick;
For me, the bully need have no respect.
Hear now, the prologue to the wretched fight
(If it's a 'fight' when you give all the blows
And I receive them all): he orders me
To stand, and I obey. What can you do
When he insists, and he's a crazy man,
And also, stronger? He starts in on me:
'Where do you come from, hey? Where did you get
That big fat belly—eating vinegar
And beans? Pfui! what cobbler asked you in
For leeks and boiled old sheepshead? Nothing to say?

18. Hideous ferryman—Charon, who rows the shades across the Styx into
the underworld.

Say something, or I'll kick you! Tell me, now,
Where do you usually beg? Some synagogue?'
Whether I try to speak, or try to go
Quietly, there's the same result: I get
A beating, then *he*'s angry, and insists
On 'bail,' before he'll let me go. This is
The 'freedom' of the poor man: having been
Beaten, he has to beg, and, cut to bits,
He prays, respectfully, to be allowed
To carry a few teeth back home with him.

"And that's not all you have to fear. When all
Is silent, and the shops are locked with chains,
Their shutters closed, there is no short supply
Of men to burglarize your locked-up house,
Or vagrants who will slit your throat with steel.
Whenever they clear out the Pomptine marsh
Or the Gallinarian forest, and set guards,
All of the undesireables rush here
As to a game preserve. What furnaces,
What anvils are not loaded up with chains?
We devote so much iron to that use,
We could run out of metal for our plows
And rakes and hoes. I think that you would say
Our ancestors were lucky, and those days
Under the kings and tribunes, which could see
The city of Rome content with just one jail!

"I could add more to what I've said, but see,
My cattle call me, and the sun declines,
It's time to go; already, several times
The mule driver has signaled with his switch.
Goodbye; remember me; and any time
Rome lets you go, to be renewed at your
Aquinum, send for me from Cumae; I'll
Visit your Helvine Ceres and Diana,
And hear your Satires, if they think me worthy,
Coming in my thick boots to your cold fields."